NEW DISCOVERIES
IN
AMERICAN QUILTS

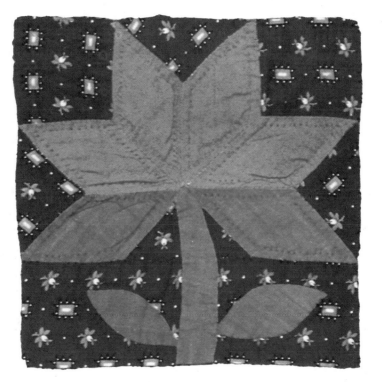

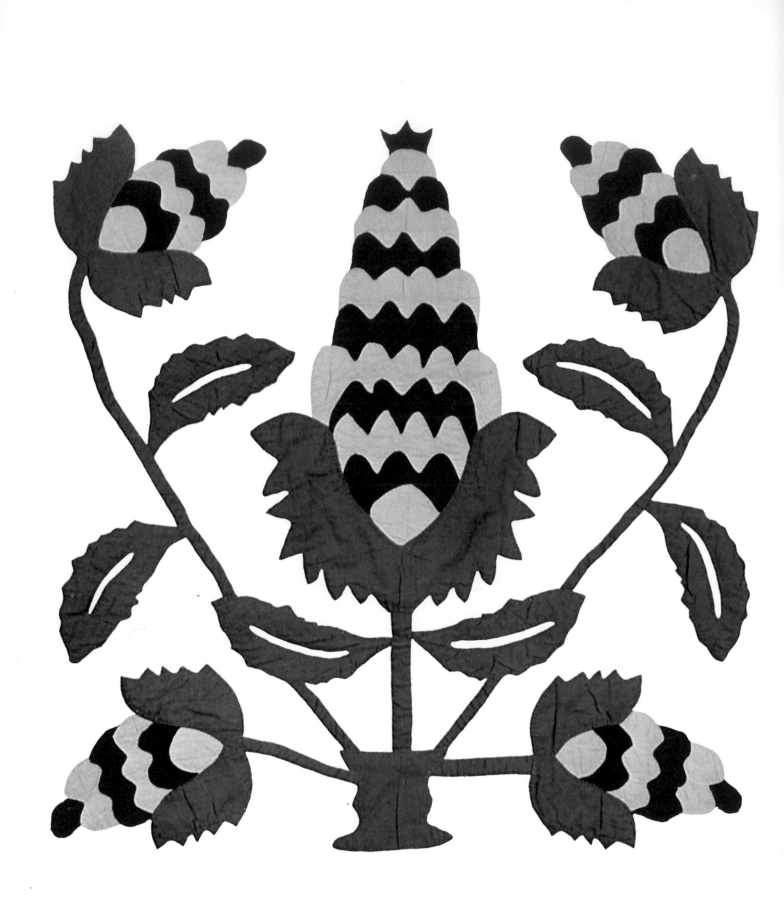

NEW DISCOVERIES IN AMERICAN QUILTS

Robert Bishop
Museum Editor
Greenfield Village and Henry Ford Museum

Patricia Coblentz
Assistant Museum Editor

NEW YORK
E. P. DUTTON & COMPANY, INC.
1975

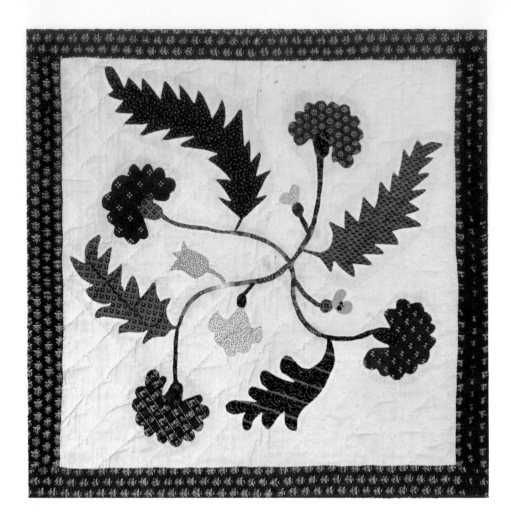

Color plate, plate 1: Enlarged detail from a pieced and appliqué quilt, Peony, Pennsylvania, c. 1895. The quilt has forty-eight squares like the one illustrated, arranged in six rows on a green background. Dimensions of whole quilt: 90″ x 75″. (Private collection; photograph courtesy Thos. K. Woodard: American Antiques & Quilts)

Color plates, above and opposite: Enlarged details from pieced and appliqué quilt, Album, Pennsylvania. The quilt is inscribed: "Barclay Reynold's Album Quilt 1853." Dimensions of whole quilt: 92″ x 92″. These two blocks from the quilt are of particular interest, for they were made in the reverse appliqué style. This type of appliqué involves cutting the design out of the background fabric, hemming the edges of the openings, and then backing the openings with the pieces of colored fabric that complete the design. (Thos. K. Woodard: American Antiques & Quilts)

Designed by Robert Bishop.

First published, 1975, in the United States by E. P. Dutton & Co., Inc., New York.
/ Published simultaneously in Canada by Clarke, Irwin & Company Limited, Toronto and Vancouver. / Printed and bound by Dai Nippon Printing Co., Ltd., Tokyo, Japan. / Library of Congress Catalog Card Number: 75-24533. / ISBN 0-525-47410-2 (DP); ISBN 0-525-16552-5 (Cloth). *First Edition*

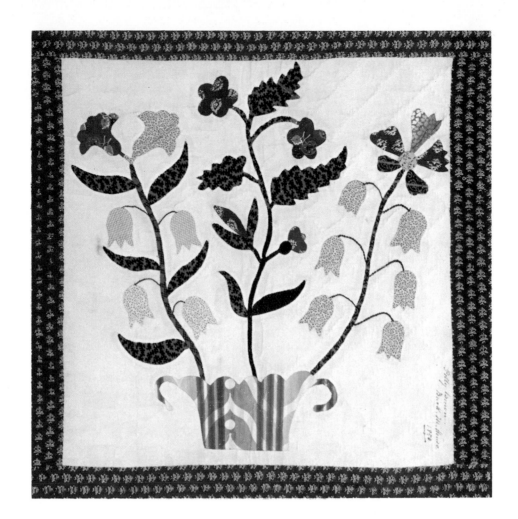

CONTENTS

ACKNOWLEDGMENTS

I wish to express my sincere gratitude to the many individuals, dealers, and institutions that have so generously provided pictorial and textual material for this book. It also gives me great pleasure to make a special acknowledgment to my editor, Cyril I. Nelson, for his expert help in bringing all the pieces together; to Patricia Coblentz, who not only served as Assistant Editor, but whose countless hours of patient reading and typing have made this book a reality; and to Barbara Black, Joan Gorman, and Martha Pike for their assistance and many valuable suggestions; and to Joel and Kate Kopp of America Hurrah Antiques for their generous help and much information. Special mention should also be made of he fine photographs provided by Arthur Vitols of Helga Photo Studio, New York, and Thomas Weddell of Cranbrook Academy, Bloomfield Hills, Michigan.

Abby Aldrich Rockefeller Folk Art Collection, Williamsburg, Virginia
Addison Gallery of American Art, Phillips Academy, Andover, Massachusetts
Adirondack Memories, Glens Falls, New York
America Hurrah Antiques, New York
The Art Institute of Chicago, Chicago, Illinois
Mr. and Mrs. Leonard Balish, Englewood, New Jersey
Baltimore County Historical Society Museum, Baltimore, Maryland
John Bihler and Henry Coger
Mr. and Mrs. John Borg
Mary Borkowski
Mr. and Mrs. Edwin Braman
Mr. and Mrs. William Burger
Chase Manhattan Bank, New York
Cincinnati Art Museum, Cincinnati, Ohio
Currier Gallery of Art, Manchester, New Hampshire
Molly Davis
Fairtree Gallery, New York
Bill Gallick and Tony Ellis, New York
Cora Ginsburg, Tarrytown, New York
Ginsburg & Levy, Inc., New York
Rhea Goodman: Quilt Gallery, Inc., New York
John Gordon, New York

Greenfield Village and Henry Ford Museum, Dearborn, Michigan
Phyllis Haders, New York
The Henry Francis du Pont Winterthur Museum, Winterthur, Delaware
Timothy and Pamela Hill, South Lyon, Michigan
Honolulu Academy of Arts, Honolulu, Hawaii
Dahlov Ipcar
Mrs. Martin Katzenberg
Mr. and Mrs. James O. Keene
Kelter-Malcé Antiques, New York
Gary and Nita Kincaid, Newburyport, Massachusetts
Malcolm Kirk
Mr. and Mrs. Bertram K. Little
Mr. and Mrs. Foster McCarl, Jr.
Mr. and Mrs. Ben Mildwoff
Mr. and Mrs. N. Richard Miller
James Mincemoyer, Sheffield, Massachusetts
Richard Miner
Mauna Kea Beach Hotel, Hawaii
Museum of Fine Arts, Boston
New York City Bicentennial Commission
Judith Pedersen and John McElhatton
Philadelphia Museum of Art, Philadelphia, Pennsylvania
The Pilgrim's Progress, New York
The Pink House, New Hope, Pennsylvania
Leo and Dorothy Rabkin
Marguerite Riordan, Stonington, Connecticut
Joanna S. Rose
Phyllis & Sidney Rosner, Scarsdale, New York
Mr. and Mrs. Henry J. Rutkowski
Patricia and James Rutkowski
George E. Schoellkopf Gallery, New York
Mrs. Samuel Schwartz
Sheldon Swope Art Gallery, Terre Haute, Indiana
Karee Skarsten
Allan Smith
Betty Sterling, Randolph, Vermont
Mary Strickler's Quilt Gallery, San Rafael, California
Lois Stulberg
Mr. and Mrs. Paul Weld
Thos. K. Woodard: American Antiques & Quilts, New York
Yale University Art Gallery, New Haven, Connecticut

INTRODUCTION

It was in 1972 that I had the pleasure of collaborating with the late Carleton L. Safford on *America's Quilts and Coverlets,* which sought to prove through several hundred illustrations the astonishing beauty of American bedcovers of all types—but mainly pieced and appliqué quilts—that have survived to the present. *America's Quilts and Coverlets* helped to increase the already strong revival of interest in these splendid examples of needlework by past generations of American women, for within the last twenty years or so all areas of both the fine and decorative arts have become more meaningful to ever-growing numbers of people. That first book had been directly inspired by the fascinating exhibition of quilts organized by Jonathan Holstein and Gail van der Hoof in 1971 at the Whitney Museum of American Art in New York City. Mr. Holstein published his own fine book on the subject in 1973, and the selected bibliography at the end of this volume lists many other works on quilts that have appeared.

The reason for this new book, *New Discoveries in American Quilts,* is simply to document as many as possible of the beautiful quilts that have been brought to my attention since 1972. Some of these are from museum collections, but the majority belong to collectors or dealers, and as many as possible have been illustrated in color. In a very few instances, quilts that first appeared in *America's Quilts and Coverlets* are repeated here so as to show them in color for the first time. Also, we have included a large selection of Amish quilts, which are so distinctive in their use of color, as well as ending the book with a group that was patriotically inspired. All of these bedcovers are fascinating, for each testifies to the individual sense of color and design possessed by its maker. In short, the American quilt has come to be recognized as a very significant contribution to the artistic expression of the American people.

Because this book may be attracting some readers to the subject for the first time, it may be useful to outline briefly the technique and development of American quilts.

During the seventeenth and eighteenth centuries most quilts were made from salvage fabrics. A woman of means could augment her bits of woolen material and linen homespun pulled from the ragbag with exotic toiles (see figure 19), brocades, damasks, and printed cottons imported from France, Italy, Sweden, England, and India. An inventory of the estate of Henry Landis, a Boston shopkeeper, taken on December 17, 1651, lists the names of over forty fabrics that could have been purchased at that time, such as: "Black Turky tamet, linsie woolsey, broadcloth, tamy cheny, adretto, herico Italiano,

sad hair coloured Italiano, say, red satinesco tufted Holland, broad dowlas, white calico."[1]

After the 1770s the vast majority of quilts were fashioned from cotton. Cambric, a finely woven linen, originally produced in Flanders, competed with the less expensive cottons—calico, chintz, dimity, gingham, and muslin.

Chintz, an imported cotton fabric, generally was printed and glazed. When it is found in an old quilt, the glazing has often disappeared through many washings. Printed designs cut from English chintzes provided colorful motifs for appliqué quilts (see figures 16 and 17).

It was not until 1793 that Eli Whitney developed the cotton gin, a machine that quickly and successfully separated cotton seeds from the blossoms. This single invention provided a base for the American textile industry.

One of the greatest benefits of the Industrial Revolution to the housewife was the mass production of inexpensive textiles. After the mid-nineteenth century, dry-goods stores carried extensive inventories of fabrics in a rainbowlike array of colors. Now materials could be purchased especially for the purpose of quiltmaking. Most attractive to the quiltmaker were the cheap cottons that were printed in several hundred different designs. No longer was quilting only a salvage art.

Quilts are generally divided into three main groups. First, there is the whole-cloth quilt that is usually made from two large pieces of fabric, one for the front and one for the back. Contrasting with it are two other major types—pieced and appliqué quilts—that together are frequently referred to as patchwork.

Several theories have been advanced toward establishing the fact that pieced quilts preceded the appliqué style. Equally convincing evidence has been used to show that appliqué quilts predate pieced examples. Actually, it seems probable that both types developed about the same time and have coexisted in beauty through the years.

Collectors are excited by quilts in several ways. Some prefer the more elaborate appliqué pieces, which are frequently further embellished by fine stitchery. The appliqué technique involves sewing a piece carefully cut from one fabric onto a ground fabric, such as an individual block, or directly onto the full-sized background fabric. After all of the appliqués have been secured to the background or the appliquéd blocks have been stitched together, the blank areas or "white spaces" left between the designs are usually quilted in decorative patterns. In some instances parts of the quilting patterns are stuffed with cotton from the back, giving a third dimension to the quilt top.

Motifs cut from the exotically designed palampores imported from India and England (see figures 14 and 15) provided appliqués that were stitched to domestically produced plain-ground fabrics. Quilts using these motifs are often said to have been fashioned in the "Broderie Perse" style. Some of the finest appliqué quilts appear to have originated in and around Baltimore, Maryland, for they share an elaborate, identifiable style. Frances Trollope, a visitor to the area, must not have seen any of these great examples of needlework, for her comments on Southern women were severe: "There is an idleness, a sauntering listlessness, that gives what we call a 'creole manner' to the fine ladies of Baltimore and Washington, which, though not quite what would be most admired, is yet infinitely more a drawing-room manner than any thing to be seen in Ohio; but I did not find that the leisure obtained by the possession of slaves was in many cases employed in the improvement of the mind. The finest ladies I saw either worked muslin or did nothing. The very trifling attempts at music are rarely continued after marriage. The drawings I saw were always most ludicrously bad, though perhaps as good as the masters', and the stock of what is called general information less than I believe any one would believe possible who had not witnessed it."[2]

Many collectors feel that the appliqué quilt lacks the inspiration of the pieced quilt and perhaps shows less inventive design, although "for show" or "best" quilts were nearly always appliqué.

Piecework produced the often stunning, even astonishing, geometric designs so popular today with collectors. The technique of piecework made it possible to achieve an almost endless variety of patterns.

Jonathan Holstein, in the introduction to his splendid book, *The Pieced Quilt: An American Design Tradition*, shares with us his enthusiasm for the pieced quilt: "I am interested more in their visual content than their craft. . . . If we strip away, then, the awe of handwork, much the awe of the sophisticate for the practical knowledge of the country or the skills of a previous time, and if we put aside the romantic associations of the quilt in American life, we can begin perhaps to see them in a different but equally meaningful way. . . . For that leaves us with surface, with pattern, color, and form."[3]

Pieced quilts were considered utilitarian and represented the everyday bedcover. They were made by sewing small, straight-edged bits of fabric together to form an overall patterned top. The designs were often contained within a series of blocks or patches that could be more easily worked. The blocks were later joined to form the quilt top.

The majority of the quilts illustrated in this book involve the pieced and the appliqué techniques. Some are a combination of the two. It is not unusual to find quilt tops made from a combination of appliquéd patches and pieced patches.

Nearly all tops were "marked" before they were quilted. Sometimes an especially skilled draftsman would attempt this difficult task freehand. More often, wooden or metal quilting blocks or templates made from cutout paper or tin (see figure 107) provided the outline that was transferred to the fabric with water-soluble ink or dye. Other times, the design was pricked into the fabric with a sharp object. When this technique was used the holes were covered by the quilting.

After a quilt top was completed, it was combined with the inner lining and backing and mounted on a quilting frame. The frame securely held the three layers and prevented them from shifting during the quilting. This was especially important, for if the material was not held tightly, the lining would puff up between the lines of stitching after washing. There were two basic types of quilting frames—one stood on legs; the other was suspended from the ceiling with pulleys.

Fine, intricate quilting was always considered one of the most important elements of a quilt. American women preferred the running stitch to the traditional backstitch generally used in Europe. Because the running stitch required less thread, it was more economical.

Some women preferred to do their own quilting. Most, however, took their handiwork to communal quilting bees, which became real social events. Even the unskilled needlewoman was invited, for her cooking talents might be used to prepare an end-of-the-day feast for the quilters.

Mrs. Trollope commented on such events: "The ladies of the Union are great workers, and, among other enterprises of ingenious industry, they frequently fabricate patchwork quilts. When the external composition of one of these is completed, it is usual to call together their neighbours and friends to witness, and assist at the *quilting*, which is the completion of this elaborate work. These assemblings are called 'quilting frolics,' and they are always solemnised with much good cheer and festivity."[4]

More personal accounts, found in diaries and journals, sometimes show that sharp needles were plied by ladies with sharp tongues: "Our minister was married a year ago, and we have been piecing him a bed quilt; and last week we quilted it. I always make a pint of going to quiltings, for you can't be backbited to your face, that's a moral sertenty . . . quiltin' just set wimmen to slanderin' as easy and beautiful as everything you ever see. So I went."[5]

The earliest American pieced quilt known is a geometric, brocaded silk and velvet example, thought to have been worked about 1704 by Sarah Sedgwick Leverett and her daughter Elizabeth. Sarah Sedgwick Leverett was the wife of John Leverett, Governor of the Massachusetts Bay Colony from 1673 to 1697. This very early quilt has a paper inner lining that includes parts of the Harvard College catalogue for 1701. The quilt has never left the Leverett-Saltonstall families since it was made, and it is currently owned by Governor and Mrs. Saltonstall of Massachusetts.

As daily life became easier and many necessities could be purchased from a store instead of produced by hand at home, leisure time increased. No longer was it necessary for quilts to be purely utilitarian. A woman could now concern herself more with the decorative aspects of her handiwork. Several years were sometimes spent on a single quilt. The name of the quilt pattern also assumed importance. Once a name was firmly established, it was handed down from one generation to the next, thus becoming a verbal tradition. As people moved about the ever-expanding country, this tradition was altered. A pattern called by one name in the East might be known by a totally different name on the western frontier. Those who have studied quilts seriously have gathered several thousand names in their efforts to categorize the multitude of patterns used by the American quiltmaker.

The names of many quilt patterns reflect regional folklore. Others indicate the religious bent of the quilter; some believed that to stitch a perfect quilt top would be an affront to God and, consequently, intentionally worked a "mistake" into the quilt. Often the Bible served as a source of names for quilt patterns. Whatever the inspiration for the naming of a pattern, one can be certain that it was meaningful to the maker, for even the simplest quilt represented a considerable investment of time and energy.

Quilts are seldom a standard size. The earliest beds were short and wide; therefore, it is not surprising that many eighteenth-century quilts are as wide as they are long. Because of improved nutrition each successive generation grew taller, and it became necessary to lengthen beds. Consequently, most quilts made after 1800 are longer than they are wide.

Nearly everyone agrees that the tradition of a young girl's attempting to fashion a "baker's dozen" quilts for her dowry is based upon actual fact. Girls were taught to sew at a very early age. One woman reminisced: "Before I was three years old, I was started at piecing a quilt. Patchwork, you know. My stint was at first only two blocks a day, but these were sewn together with the greatest care or they were unraveled and done over. Two blocks was called 'a single,' but when I got a little bigger I had to make two pairs of singles and sew the four blocks together, and I was pretty proud when I had finished them . . ."[6]

Young girls learned to piece quilts first, then make the more difficult appliqués, before finally attempting the "wedding" or thirteenth quilt, which would usually be either an elaborate, intricately stitched, appliquéd quilt or an equally handsome all-white spread intended for her wedding bed.

But quilting was not solely a feminine art. A few rare examples of quilts made by men have come to light. The great collection at Vermont's Shelburne Museum has a pictorial quilt made by a Civil War veteran, and figure 93 in this book shows a stunning pieced quilt of the Log Cabin type made by a tailor at the end of the nineteenth century in New York City. Also, in *The Romance of the Patchwork Quilt in America* we are told the following: ". . . once in a blue moon, one finds a man who is fascinated with the artistic possibilities of the patchwork quilt. Such a man is Charles Pratt . . . He claims to be the champion quilter of the whole world, having in his possession over two hundred letters which testify to his supremacy in his chosen field. He goes from state to state, to exhibit his prize quilts, and has 393 prizes to his credit."[7]

For many, the genius of the American quilt lies in its value as an American cultural artifact. Others believe that the often incredibly beautiful quilt-top designs are the most significant aspect. There are also those who will argue that, after all, it is the needlework that counts most.

For me, the beauty of American quilts is all of these, and more besides.

I remember as a young child visiting my grandmother's white clapboard, Cape Cod-style farmhouse in Maine. Those were the war years, and both food and money were scarce. Like so many accomplished women before her, she made the quilts for all the family beds.

Because I slept in the attic, I was given more quilts than anyone else. During the coldest months as many as five quilts were piled on top of my bed. They were not made from homespun materials but from carefully washed and bleached grain bags. My favorite, and the warmest I might add, was resplendent with brilliant orange poppies appliquéd on a bleached muslin background.

Anyone who has snuggled under such a bedcover knows that the real beauty of a quilt comes from the happiness, security, and warmth that its loving maker has stitched into her creation.

ROBERT BISHOP

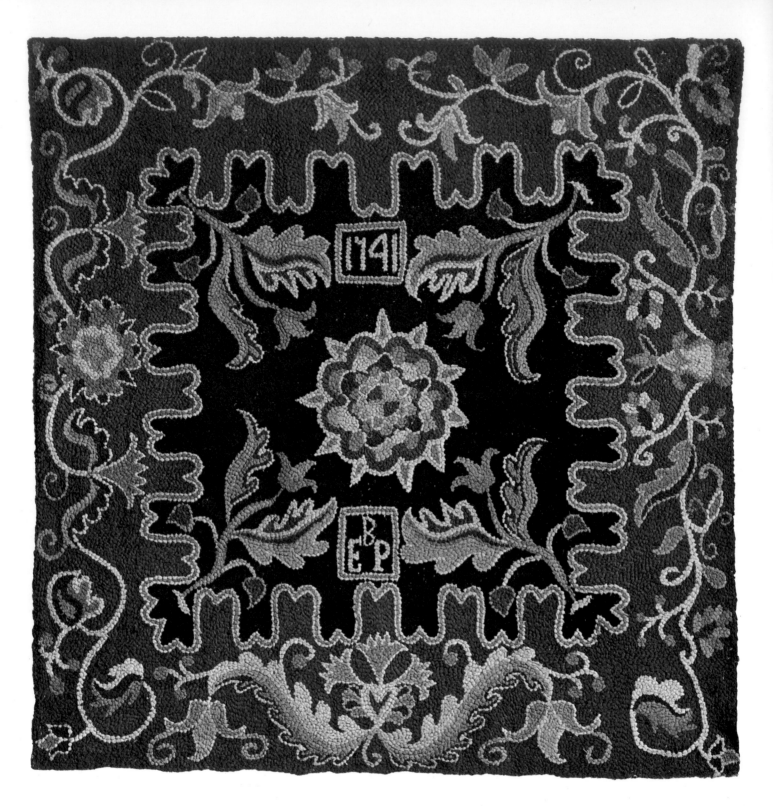

1 (above). Bed rug made by Phoebe Billings, dated 1741 and initialed ᴇ ᴮ ᴘ. 96″ x 96″. This handsome example of unusual design and color is worked with a running stitch; the pile is uncut. The earliest bed rug known is in the collection of the Essex Institute at Salem, Massachusetts. It is inscribed MA for Mary Avery, its maker, and dated 1722. Many American bed rugs are initialed and dated, which is not surprising for they represented countless hours of patient labor. (Addison Gallery of American Art, Phillips Academy)

2 (opposite). Bed rug made by Hannah Johnson (1770–1818), dated 1796 and initialed HJ. 98″ x 94″. The number 26 beneath the date indicates Hannah's age at the time she made the rug. She used a running stitch and then cut the pile. The elaborate designs of many bed rugs that are based on a vase of flowers and flower-and-leaf meander, of which this is a typical example, were probably not original creations. The patterns derive from the cotton coverlets, imported from India and popular in England during the late seventeenth century, which included Tree-of-Life designs and ornate floral motifs. (The Art Institute of Chicago; Gift of The Needlework and Textile Guild)

THE BED RUG

Bed rugs—the handsome, heavy wool bedcovers made in New England (chiefly in Connecticut) during the eighteenth and early nineteenth centuries—were completely a home production. Wool was sheared, then washed, carded, spun, and finally dyed with natural dyes. Home-woven wool or linen was the base fabric on which bold designs were worked in thick, colorful, woolen yarns with a wood or bone needle. The majority of bed rugs have a looped surface pile that is sometimes sheared.

Bed rugs are probably the rarest form of American bedcovers. In the catalogue, *Bed Ruggs/1722–1833*, of the 1972 landmark exhibition of bed rugs organized by William L. Warren at the Wadsworth Atheneum, Hartford, Connecticut, only forty-one rugs are illustrated.

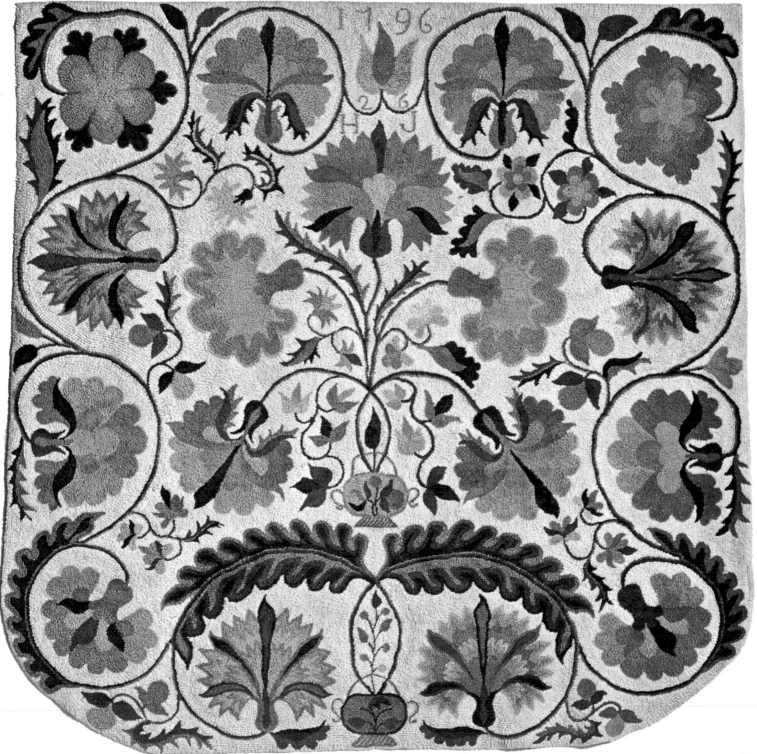

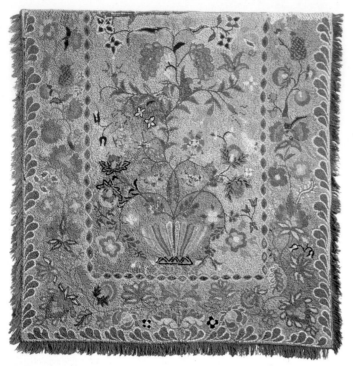

6 (opposite). The bed in old red paint with its splendid bed rug is the focal point for this handsome New England room. The bed rug was made with a darning stitch. It is initialed LM and dated 1821. 108″ x 102″. (Private collection)

5 (below). Bed rug, dated 1771. 90″ x 78″. A darning stitch was used to create this delightfully rustic version of the Tree-of-Life pattern on a natural wool foundation. (Currier Gallery of Art)

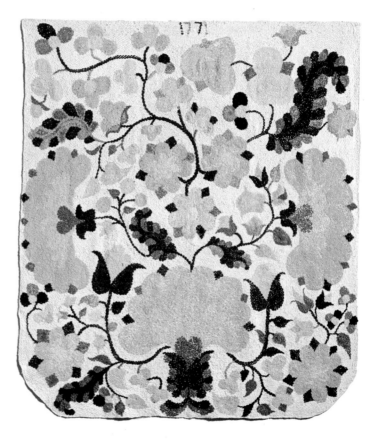

3 (above). Bed rug made by Deborah Loomis Brace (1752–1839), dated 1772 and initialed DB. 87″ x 86″. This bed rug is worked on a natural wool foundation in a running stitch and the pile was cut. The amount of yarn needed for a bed rug was carefully calculated in advance since it was almost impossible to duplicate a color in a second dye lot. (Yale University Art Gallery; Mabel Brady Garvan Collection)

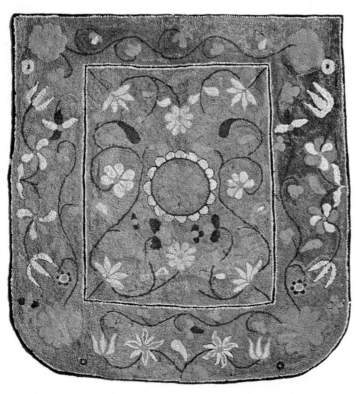

4 (left). Bed rug made by Hannah Baldwin, dated 1741. 85¼″ x 79″. Made with a running stitch on wool foundation. The pile is both cut and uncut. At one time bed rugs were thought to be hooked; it is now known that the majority were yarn-sewn with a running or darning stitch and that the hooking technique was never used. The individuality of this piece shows that Hannah Baldwin probably relied upon her own imagination for the motifs. (Mr. and Mrs. Paul Weld)

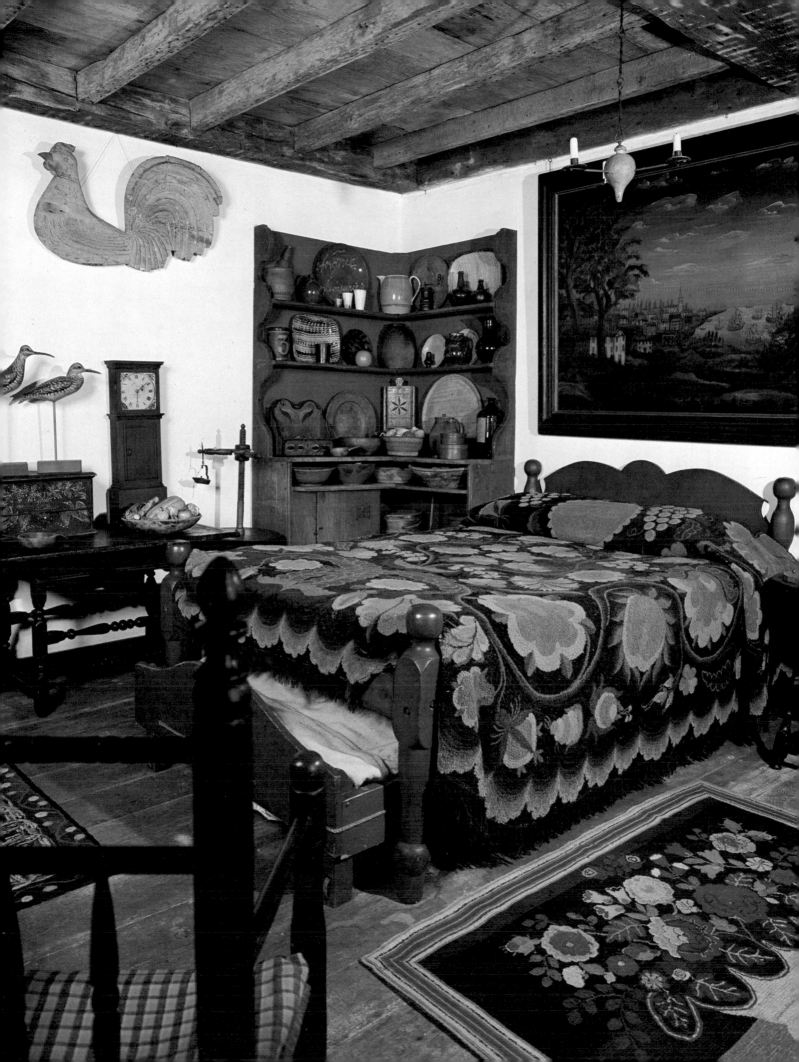

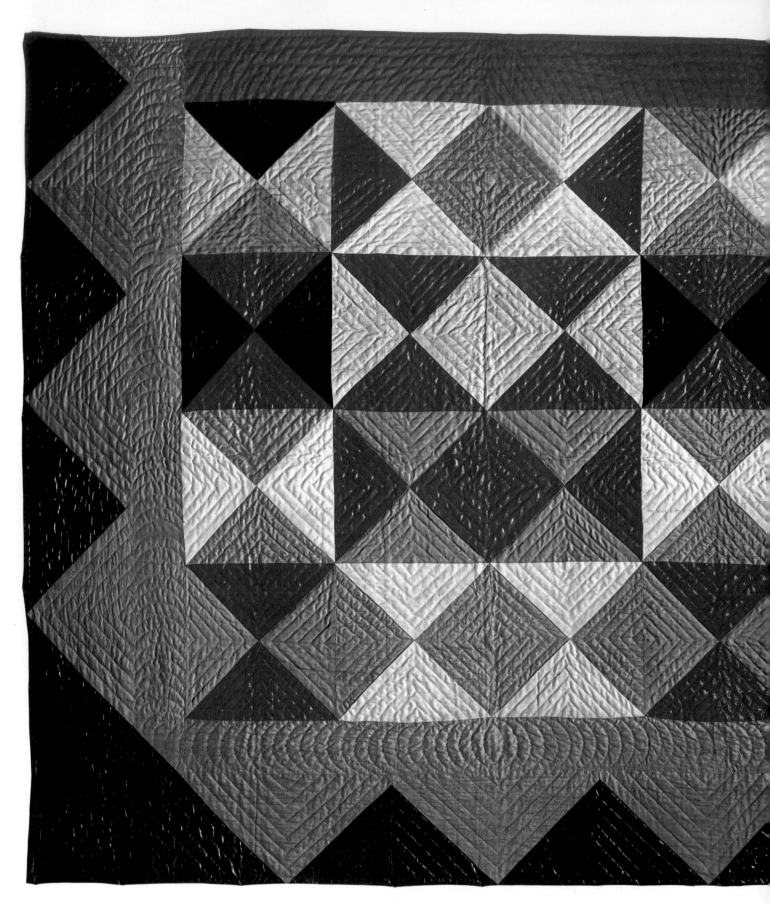

7 (above). Pieced quilt of glazed linsey-woolsey, harlequin design, New England, 1800–1820. 86¾″ x 96″. Linsey-woolsey was usually made into whole-cloth spreads fashioned from one or two pieces of fabric. As the bedcover wore out, fragments in good condition were salvaged and later made into pieced quilts like this extraordinary example. (Private collection; photograph courtesy George E. Schoellkopf Gallery)

LINSEY-WOOLSEY

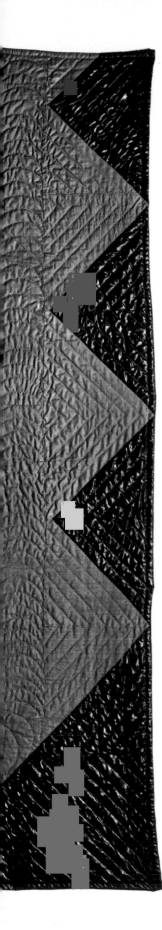

Linsey-woolsey was first made in England and derives its name from Linsey, a village in Sussex. This coarse, loosely woven fabric was generally made of a linen warp and wool weft; however, cotton was occasionally substituted for linen, which is derived from the flax plant.

Nearly as soon as the first Colonists cleared their land, flax seeds were sown. With the exception of food, flax contributed more toward the establishment of permanent settlements than any other crop. It was planted early in the spring and matured in late June or July. It was pulled from the ground and left to dry thoroughly. After the several processes of ripping, retting, breaking, scutching, and hatcheling, it was possible to remove long fibers from the woody stock. These were then dressed on a distaff and spun into thread. The thread was subsequently bleached in ashes and water, rinsed, washed, dyed, and finally wound onto the bobbins and shuttles of a loom where it was woven into a strong, durable fabric.

Linsey-woolsey is one of the earliest and handsomest types of American quilted bedcovers, and like the bed rug, it was especially treasured in cold climates.

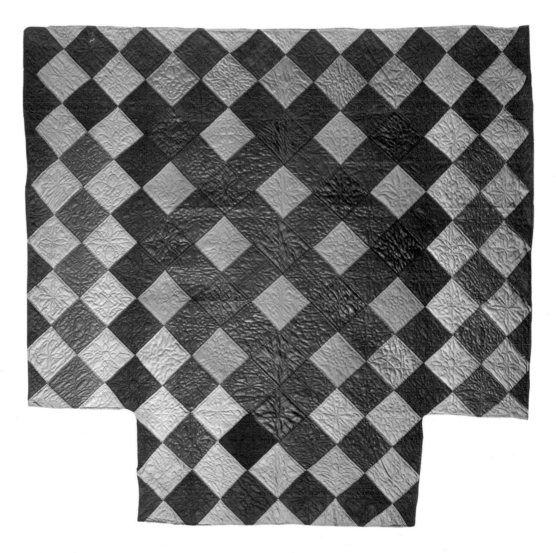

8 (above). Pieced quilt of glazed linsey-woolsey, harlequin design, New England, c. 1800. 99½″ x 104″. Floral motifs have been quilted into the rectangular blocks of this striking bedcover. (Cora Ginsburg)

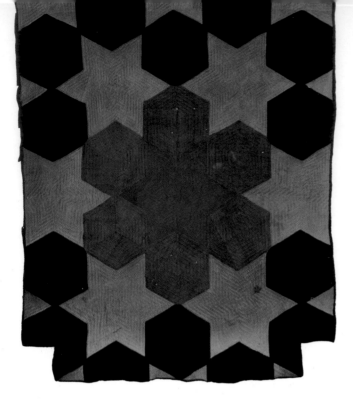

9 (left). Pieced linsey-woolsey in a pattern of stars and hexagons, New England, c. 1800. 76½" x 70". The quilting follows the general outline of the pieces: the stars are quilted in a star design; the hexagons are quilted in a hexagonal pattern. (Gary and Nita Kincaid)

10 (below). Pieced linsey-woolsey, New England, c. 1780. 88¼" x 86". The borders are quilted in a handsome, undulating feather pattern, and the central panel features a large heart. (Mr. and Mrs. Foster McCarl, Jr.)

11 (opposite). The curly maple bed in this room is covered with a glazed linsey-woolsey quilt made in New York about 1800. 101" x 99". The eight-pointed star, called Variable Star, was a favorite motif with quilters. This beautiful spread is elaborately quilted with large hearts and the feather design. (Private collection)

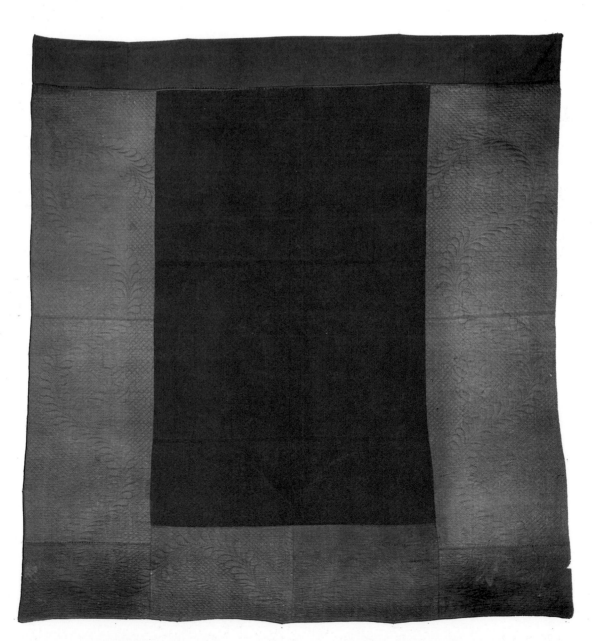

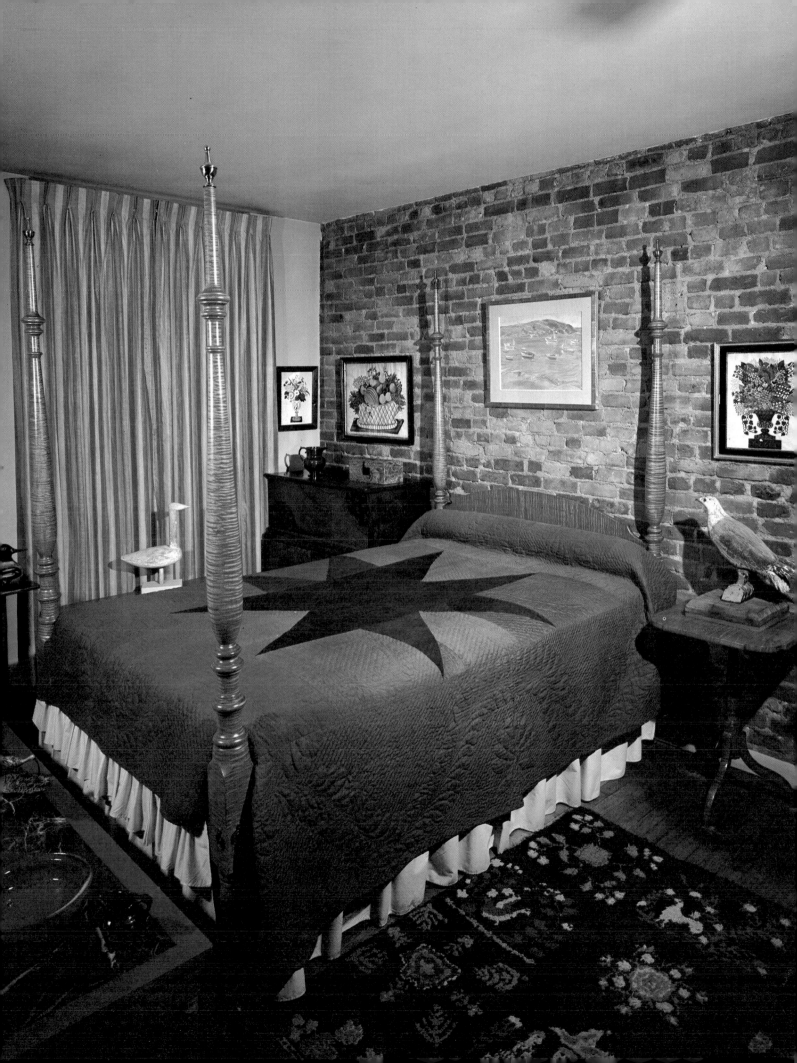

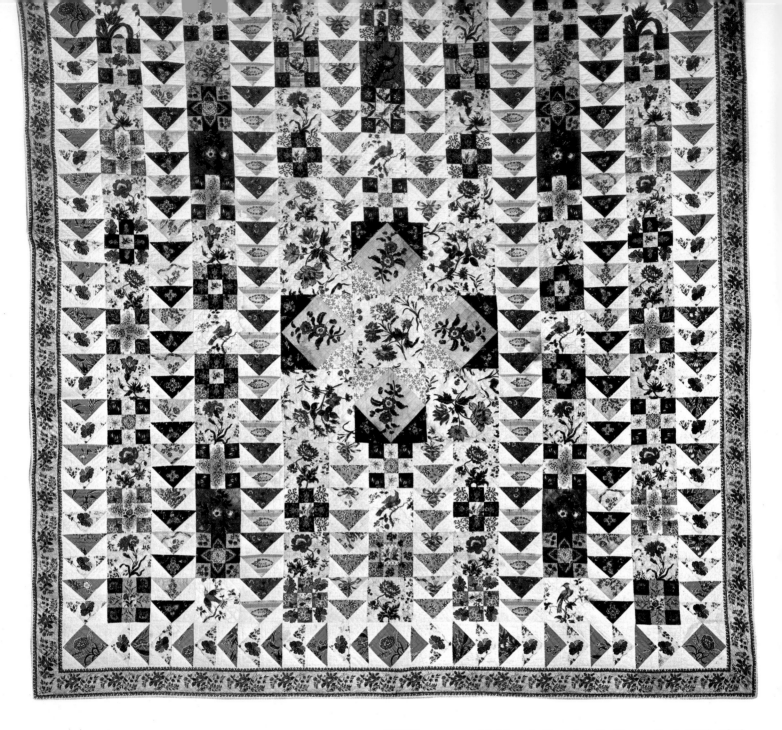

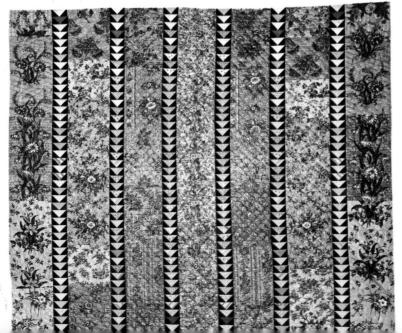

12 (above). Pieced quilt, Connecticut, 1820–1830. 100" x 100". Chintz pieces printed with floral and bird motifs have been incorporated into the overall design of this marvelous quilt. The central nine-patch medallion incorporates a Variable Star. Strips made with Flying Geese patches alternate with strips using plain and nine-patch blocks. The quilt has an edging of handwoven tape. (Private collection; photograph courtesy Thos. K. Woodard: American Antiques & Quilts)

13 (left). Pieced quilt, New England, 1820–1825. 106" x 111½". This is another splendid example of a quilt created from bars made of chintz blocks alternating with strips in the Flying Geese pattern. The quilt is embroidered with twenty sets of initials. (The Pink House)

THE WHOLE-CLOTH SPREAD

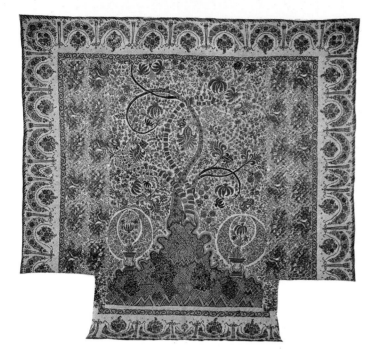

14 (above). Palampore, Indian export, Maine, c. 1835. 111" x 84". This richly ornamental spread, made in India with the mordant-dyeing technique, was widened by inserting panels of English chintz between the central section and the garlanded borders. (Cora Ginsburg)

15 (below). Palampore, Indian export, c. 1775. 116" x 78". Made with the resist-dyeing and mordant-dyeing techniques, this eighteenth-century spread features the Tree-of-Life design, as does figure 14. (Ginsburg & Levy, Inc.)

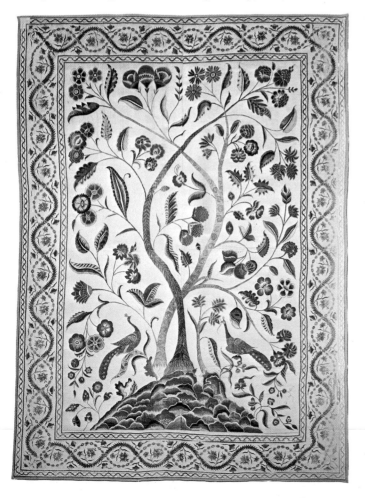

During the late seventeenth and early eighteenth centuries the American taste for printed fabrics was a reflection of English fashion. The ships of the East India trading companies returned from the Orient to English seaports laden with hand-colored cottons. Many of these were exported to the American Colonies. Their fast-dyed, vibrant colors brightened life in the Colonial settlements that dotted the eastern seaboard.

English and French textile printers quickly began to copy the Indian designs and their products also enjoyed an immense popularity in America. Many of these imported textiles first saw service as dresses, curtains, and bed furniture. As they wore out, the good remnants often became part of a quilt or bedcover.

During the last twenty years of the seventeenth century numerous orders for printed palampores, or bedcovers, were sent to India by English and American merchants. Diaries from this period indicate that some palampores reached America, where examples with "Grounds green, purple, red and some white, with variety of painting, curious and lively brisk colors"[8] earned for prosperous housewives the envy of their neighbors.

During the eighteenth century English cottons printed with naturalistic floral and bird designs cornered the American market. After the Revolution, French toiles with pictorial landscapes and classical vignettes became popular as well. At the close of the eighteenth century printed fabrics were also manufactured in America.

Designs were printed on fabrics in three ways. The earliest technique involved the use of wooden blocks that had engraved patterns on their surfaces. A separate block was required for each motif. By the very nature of the process designs remained relatively simple.

A second technique involving the use of an engraved copper plate became popular after 1750. The designs of copperplate-printed fabrics are invariably of a single color laid on a white or neutral background.

Soon after the opening of the nineteenth century roller printing or "machined goods" began to reduce greatly the cost of printed fabrics. With the abundance of inexpensive printed textiles that resulted quilts made from multicolored fabrics appeared in quantity. By 1836 machine-printed textiles had become so plentiful that Sir Edward Baines, writing in his *History of the Cotton Manufacture in Great Britain*, noted: "The humblest class has now the means of as great neatness and even gaiety of dress as the middle and upper classes of the last age. A country wake of the nineteenth century may display as much finery as a drawing-room of the eighteenth; and the peasant's cottage may at this day with good management have as handsome furniture [furnishings] for beds, windows and tables as the house of a substantial tradesman sixty years ago."[9]

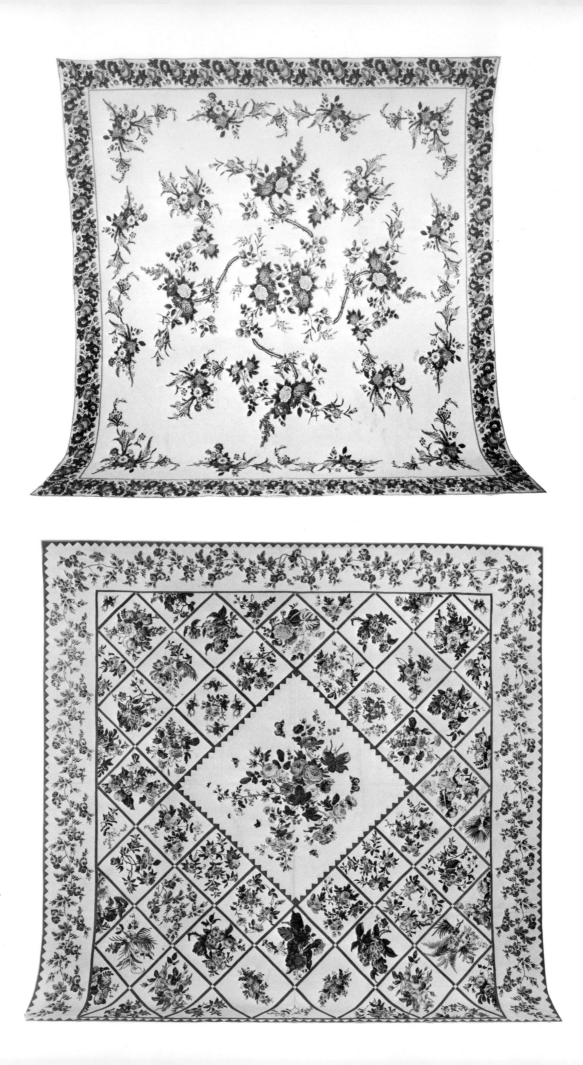

16 (opposite, above). Some of the handsomest bedcovers that have survived are those created by cutting the printed motifs out of English chintzes and then sewing them to a backing of fine cotton. As can be seen from the elegant appliqué quilts shown on page 20, this involved expert and exacting needlework. One helpful instruction book published in 1882 recommended: "Stretch your background upon a frame, and paste the chintz flowers into position upon it. When the pasting is finished and dry, take the work out of the frame and stitch loosely with as little visibility as possible, all around the leaves and flowers."[10] (Mr. and Mrs. Leonard Balish)

17 (opposite, below). Appliqué quilt, Wilmington, Delaware, area, c. 1820. 111″ x 109″. Note how the floral designs in figure 16 have been appliquéd to form a large central medallion with a swirling movement, while the motifs of birds, cupids, roses, butterflies, and ferns in this illustration are all beautifully framed. (Mr. and Mrs. Leonard Balish)

18 (below). Pieced quilt, New England, c. 1835. 100″ x 98″. The soft tones of the borders frame bars of boldly patterned, brightly colored English chintz. (America Hurrah Antiques)

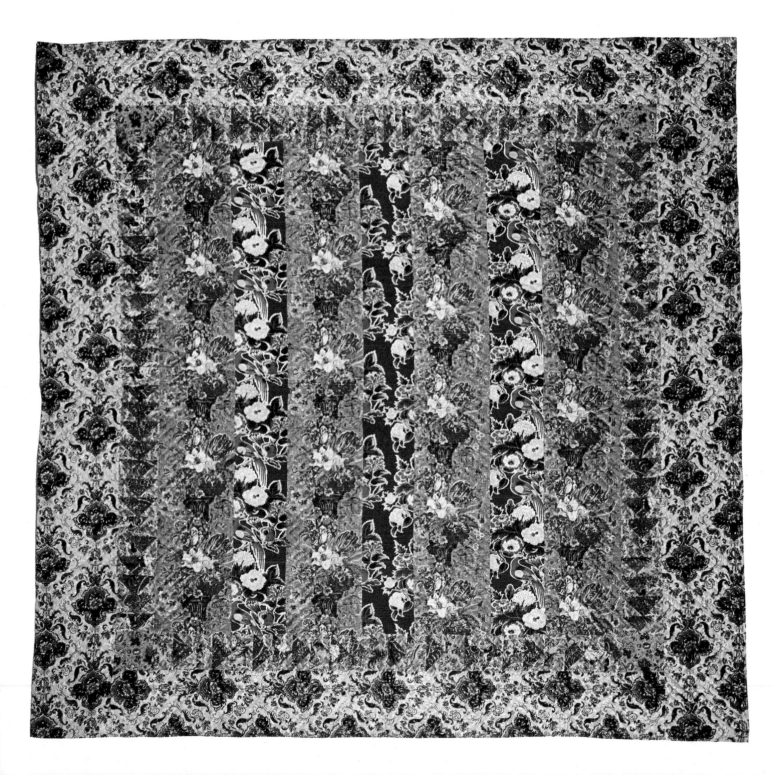

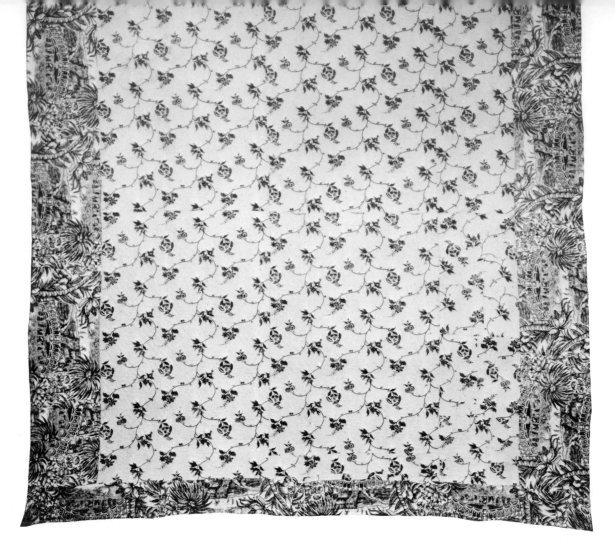

19 (above), 19a (below). Bedcover with a block-printed floral center and a copperplate border, 1800–1810. 92″ x 92″. The printed border has a repeat design that features (above the center) an Indian kidnapping a white child. On the right side of the ornate bridge in the foreground two white settlers are seen pursuing the red man. The native American never ceased to pique the curiosity of eighteenth-century Europeans. Five Iroquois chiefs caused a sensation at the English court when they were taken by Captain Peter Schuyler, head commissioner of Indian Affairs for New York, to visit Queen Anne in 1710. (America Hurrah Antiques)

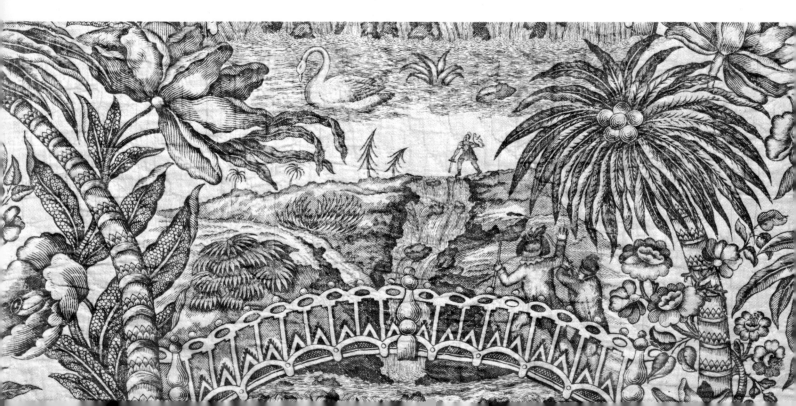

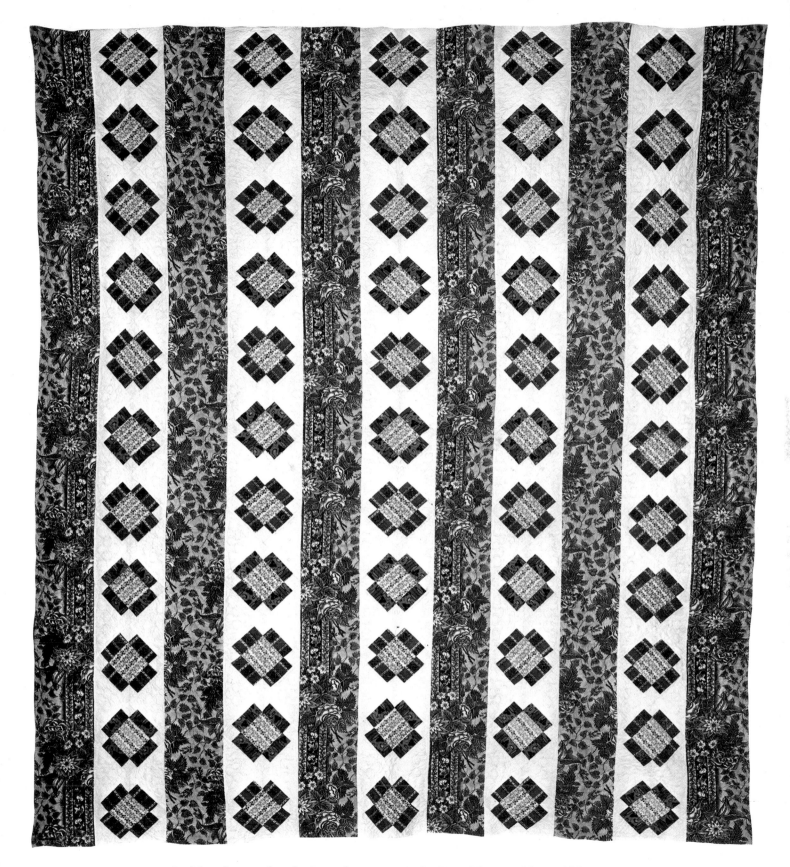

20 (above). Pieced quilt, Pennsylvania, c. 1837. 106" x 95". Broad bars of blue
chintz, which is possibly French in origin, are combined here with pieced squares
of polychrome cotton. A card dated 1912 that was pinned to the quilt states:
"This quilt was made for Christian Ihman, New Holland, Pennsylvania, 75 years
ago." (Private collection; photograph courtesy George E. Schoellkopf Gallery)

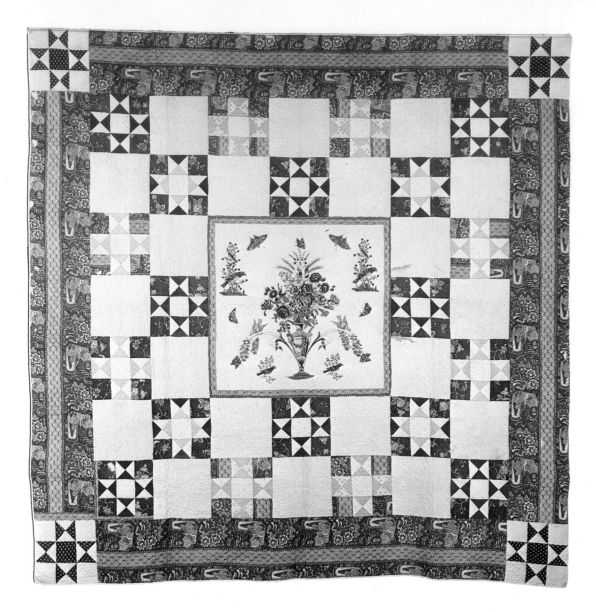

21 (above). Pieced quilt with a central medallion printed by John Hewson, dated 1811. 92" x 93". Central medallion measures 28" x 28½". Blocks of eight-pointed Variable Stars alternate with plain blocks and are used to form the four corners of this exciting quilt. (Cincinnati Art Museum; Gift of Mary Louise Burton)

22 (opposite, above). Pieced quilt made by Zibiah Smallwood, wife of John Hewson, from pieces printed by her husband, Philadelphia, 1800. 104" x 102". (Philadelphia Museum of Art; Gift of Miss Ella Hodgson, great-granddaughter of John Hewson)

Perhaps no American textile printer has achieved the fame of John Hewson, who opened a printing manufactory and bleaching yard at Gunner's River, Pennsylvania, in 1774. Hewson, an English emigrant, owed much of his success to America's political and social leaders. Benjamin Franklin, meeting Hewson on a trip abroad, encouraged him to settle in the Colonies; Martha Washington wore gowns made from his printed cottons.

In the Grand Federal Procession of 1788 celebrating the adoption of the United States Constitution, Hewson represented the Pennsylvania Society for the Encouragement of Manufactures and the Useful Arts. His thirty-foot-long float, drawn by several handsome horses, excited a local newspaper to observe admiringly: "Behind the looms was fixed the apparatus of Mr. Hewson, printing muslins of an elegant chintz pattern, and Mr. Lang, designing and cutting prints for shauls; on the right was seated Mrs. Hewson and her 4 daughters, pencilling a piece of very neat sprigged chintz of Mr. Hewson's printing, all dressed in cottons of their own manufacture; on the back of the carriage, on a lofty staff, was displayed the callico printer's flag, in the center 13 stars in a blue field, and thirteen red stripes in a white field; round the edges of the flag was printed 37 different prints of various colours, one of them a very elegant bed-furniture chintz of six colours, as specimens of printing done at Philadelphia."[11]

Hewson's printed fabrics represent the finest known American textile printing of the eighteenth century. Quilts incorporating his beautiful designs are very rare.

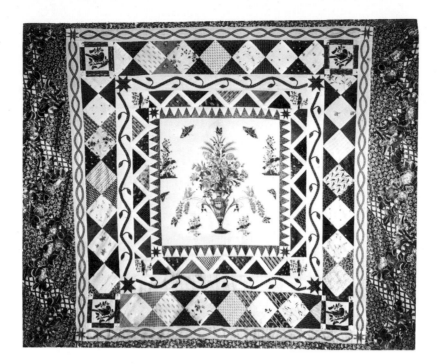

23 (below). Printed cotton bedspread attributed to John Hewson, Philadelphia, 1780–1800. 106¼″ x 103¼″. Only two complete spreads printed by John Hewson are known. (The Henry Francis du Pont Winterthur Museum)

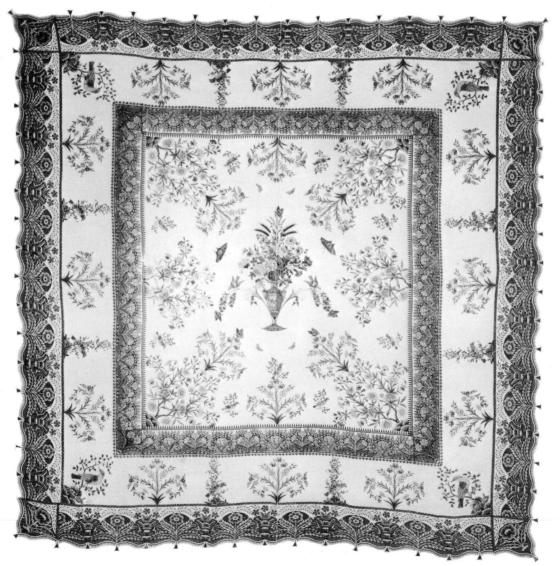

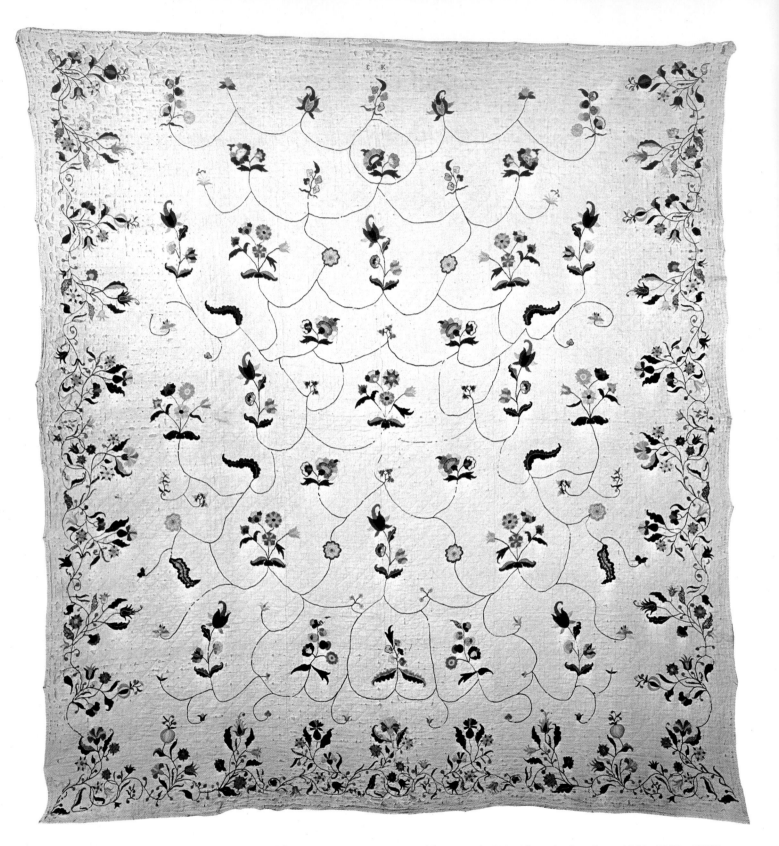

24 (above). Bedcover of crewel-embroidered linen, Boston, 1760–1770. 96″ x 84½″. Initialed at top EK for Emily Knight. This lovely, rhythmic composition features single blossoms and groups of flowers and leaves sinuously interconnected with tendrils. (Cora Ginsburg)

25 (opposite). Crewel-worked quilt, c. 1810. 91½″ x 70½″. Blocks of English pillar-printed cotton alternate with white muslin blocks that have been handsomely crewel embroidered. The lower corners of the quilt have been cut to fit the footposts of a bed. (Mrs. Martin Katzenberg)

THE "WORKT" SPREAD

Crewel, which was undoubtedly a major creative outlet for the Colonial woman, was usually "workt" or embroidered on linen homespun. Floral designs were especially popular during the eighteenth century, and many show the influence of imported Oriental fabrics and older Jacobean embroidery. Other motifs were inspired by the direct observation of nature.

Almost from the beginning of the Colonial period pattern books, such as Richard Schorleyker's *A Scholo-House for the Needle*, published in London in 1632, provided information for those who needed to "live by the needle and give good content to adorne the worthy."[12] This publication was profusely illustrated with motifs that often appear in American crewel work.

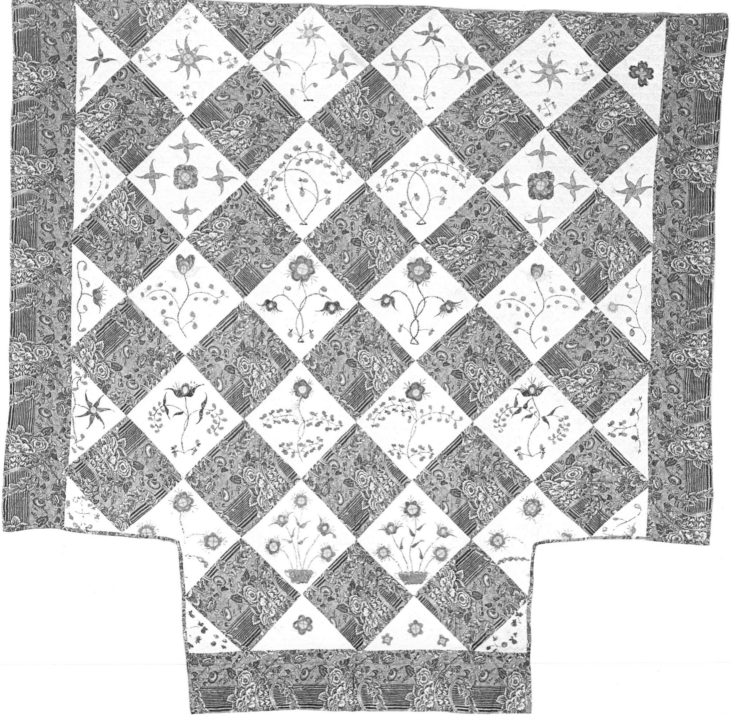

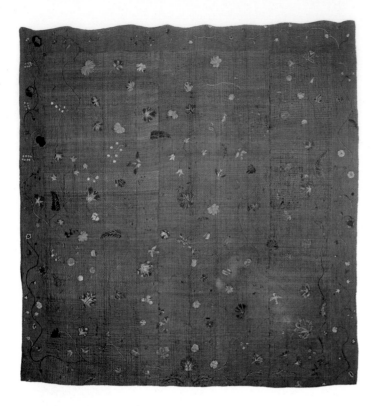

26 (above). Linsey-woolsey bedcover with crewel embroidery, New England, c. 1775. 88″ x 85″. This smashing country piece scatters its blooms randomly over the surface, in contrast to the more refined orderliness of the bouquets in the spread on the opposite page. (James Mincemoyer)

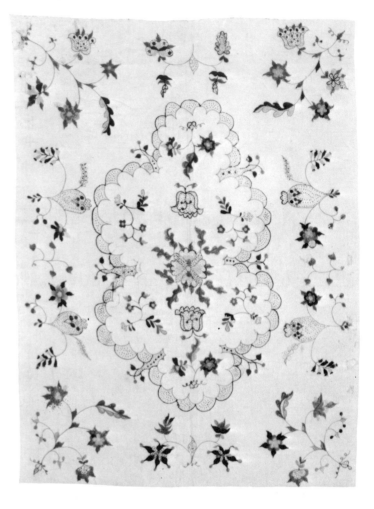

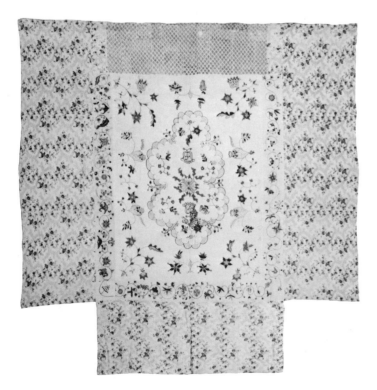

27 (left), 27a (above). Linen coverlet with crewel embroidery, c. 1760. 96½″ x 94″. The drops are of printed cotton that have been quilted. (Greenfield Village and Henry Ford Museum)

28 (below). Bedcover of black wool embroidered with a beautifully designed garden of flowers sprouting from baskets, including daisies, roses, and carnation, c. 1770. 96" x 80". Wool was a great luxury in early America, and obtaining fast dyes for crewel yarns was also difficult. One gentleman complained about the great cost of dye in America just after the Revolution. "For a great proportion, the ingredients employed in dyes, we depend on Europe to furnish . . . as we attempt an independence of their markets, they increase their duties on dyestuffs which we import. Not one cask of cochineal, can we obtain from our sister continent, South Africa; from thence it must pop through the hands of Spain and England . . ."[13] (Greenfield Village and Henry Ford Museum)

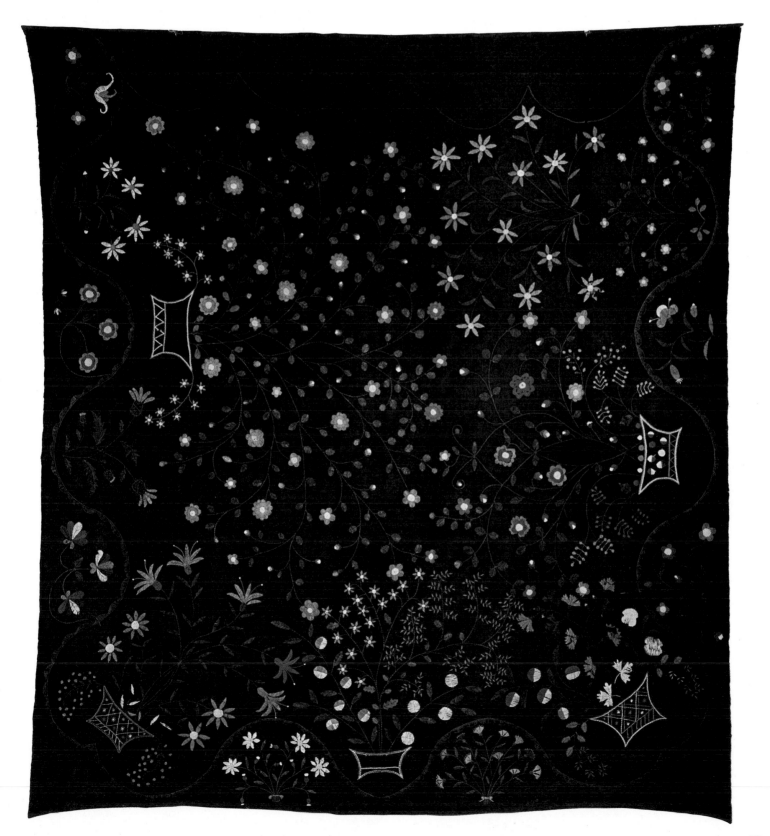

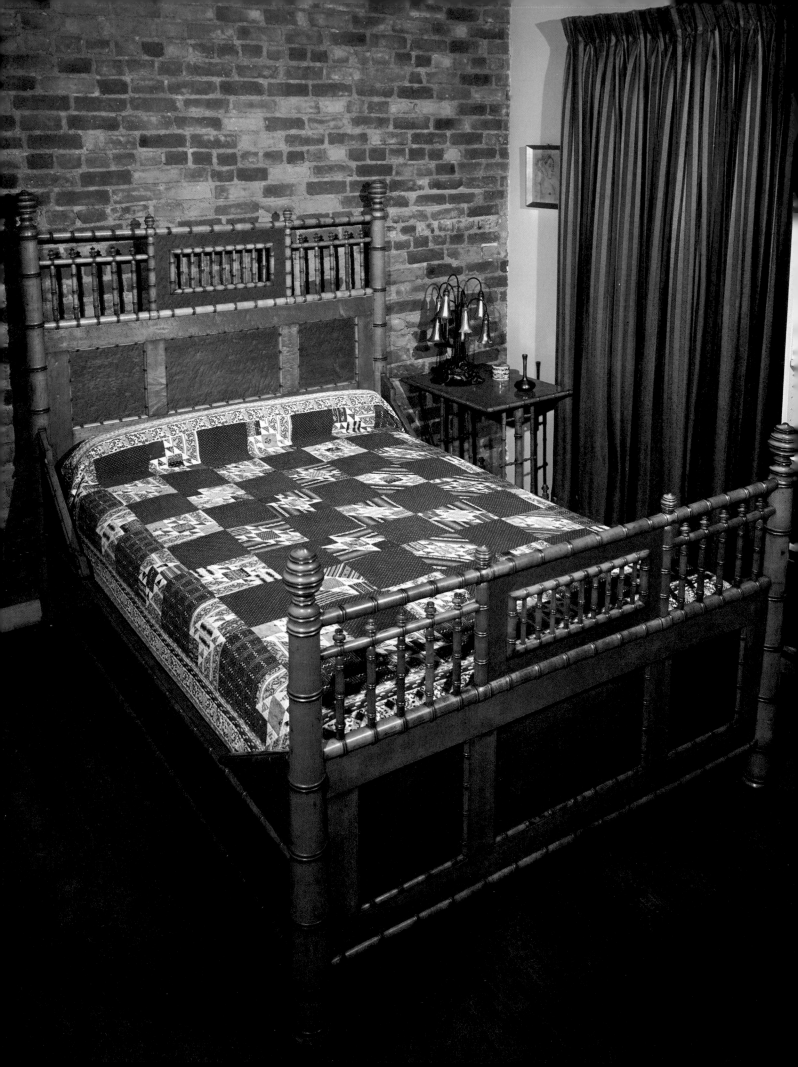

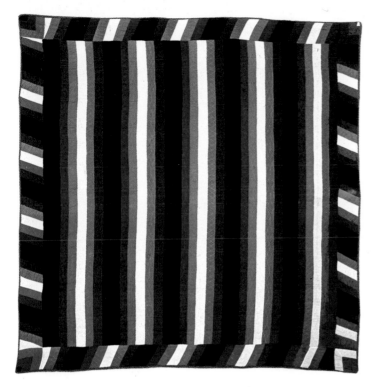

THE PIECED QUILT

As is true of other branches of American folk art, like painting and sculpture, it was during the nineteenth century that the art of the pieced quilt exploded with the sheer energy of creativity. The women of that time have bequeathed posterity a priceless legacy of beauty made, in many cases, from only remnants of fabric. Today we can only marvel at the seemingly endless hours devoted to producing what are in so many cases masterworks of color, design, and needlework. Words really cannot do justice to what has been accomplished in the majority of these quilts; ultimately they must speak for themselves. They do so eloquently.

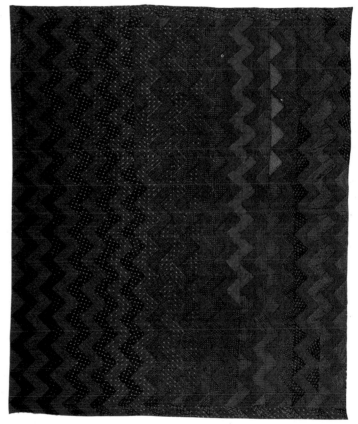

29 (opposite). Pieced quilt, Pennsylvania, 1840–1850. 91¼" x 85¾". The richly colored quilt covers a bed made about 1905 of maple turned to simulate Oriental bamboo. A lily-pad lamp and vase made by Louis C. Tiffany are on the matching maple table. (Private collection)

30 (above). Pieced quilt, Joseph's Coat, Pennsylvania, c. 1875. 84" x 80". When quilts of this type are framed by an outside border, they are generally referred to as Joseph's Coat. Those without a border, like figure 31, are often called Rainbow. (Phyllis Haders)

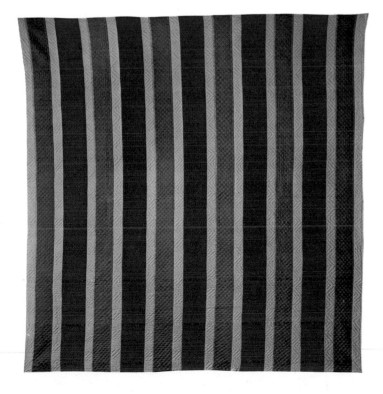

31 (left). Pieced quilt, Rainbow, Pennsylvania, 1870–1875. 83" x 80". (America Hurrah Antiques)

32 (above). Pieced quilt, Streak o' Lightning, 1870–1880. 87" x 72¾". Red and blue cottons of several patterns and colors have been combined in this effective quilt. (George E. Schoellkopf Gallery)

33 (below). Pieced quilt made in 1848 by Maria Cadman Hubbard at the age of 79. Probably New England. 88½" x 81½". We can only be in awe of the devout spirit that impelled Maria Hubbard to create this masterwork. The pious sayings are constructed of tiny squares of material pieced together, and all are contained within a strong, handsome design of sawtoothed triangles, squares, and diamonds. (Private collection; photograph courtesy George E. Schoellkopf Gallery)

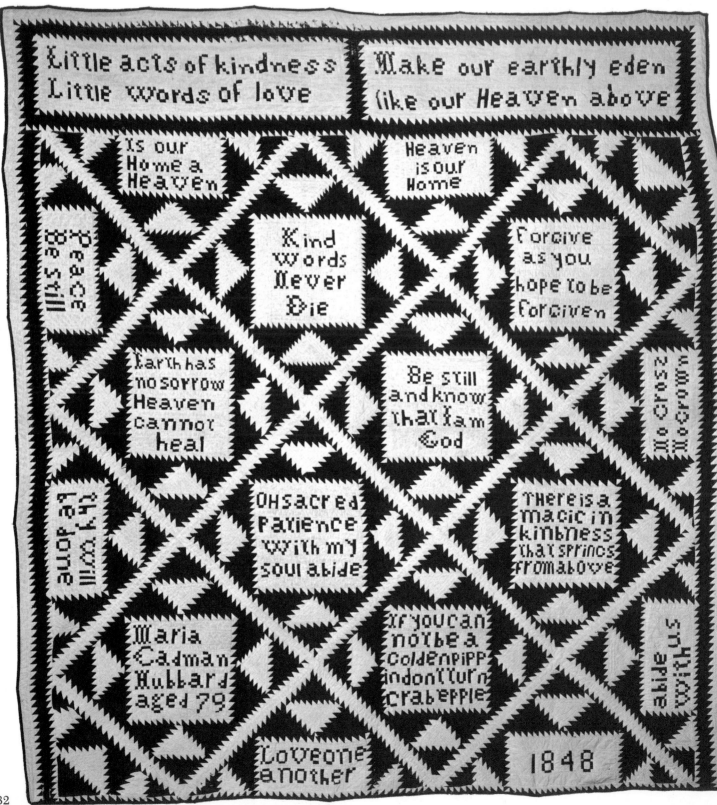

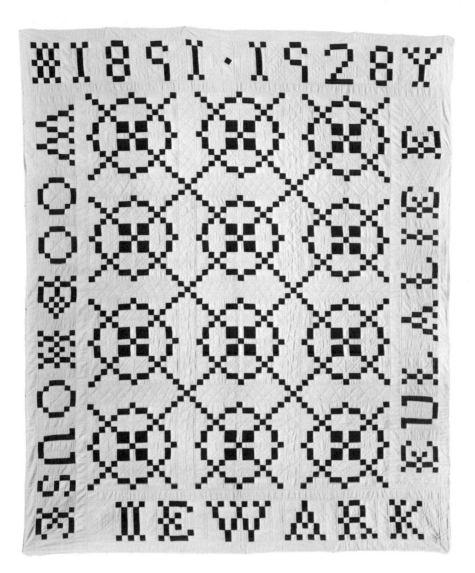

34 (above). Pieced quilt signed Eulalie E. Woodhouse, Newark, and dated 1891–1928. It is probable that this handsome red-and-white quilt, based on the Burgoyne Surrounded pattern, was finished in 1928. The design of the center is quite similar to that found on drafts or weaving patterns for coverlets. (The Pink House)

35 (right). Pieced alphabet quilt top made with red letters on a blue background, Pennsylvania, c. 1900. 87″ x 79″. This piece was undoubtedly made for a child, and the building in the lower right corner is surely a schoolhouse. (Kelter-Malcé Antiques)

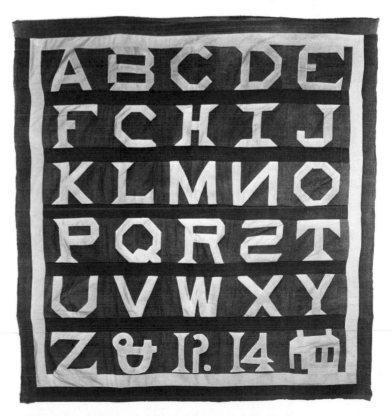

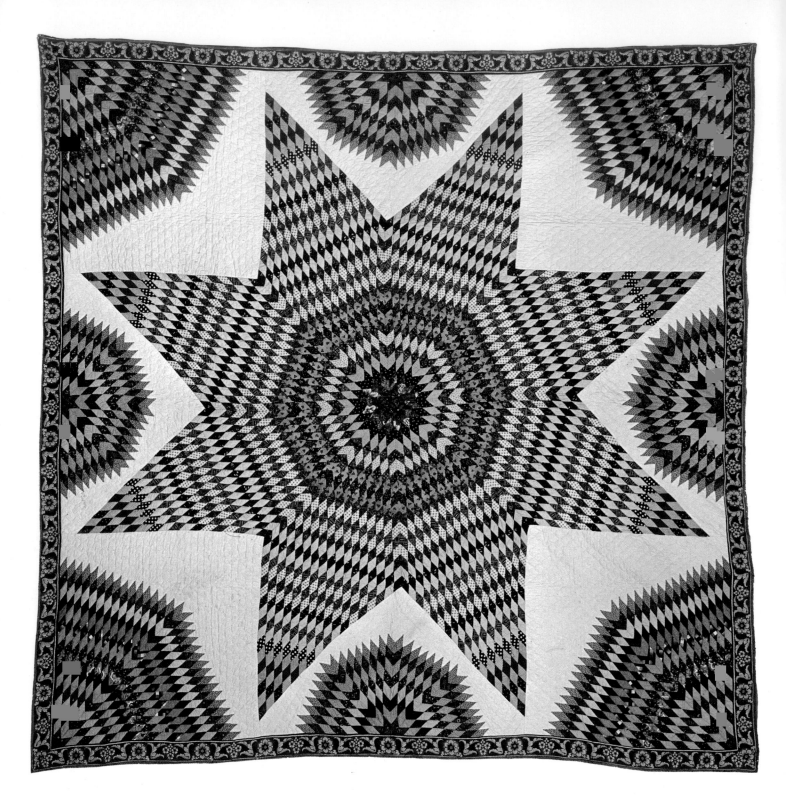

36 (above). Pieced quilt, Star of Bethlehem, made by Elizabeth E. Moseman, Port Chester, New York, c. 1849. 92″ x 90¾″. Half sunbursts are used as decorative motifs on the four sides, and quarter sunbursts embellish the corners. This brilliant quilt won first prize at the State Fair held at Bridgeport, Connecticut, in the year it was made. It contains 4,212 pieces. (Chase Manhattan Bank; photograph courtesy America Hurrah Antiques)

37 (opposite, above left). Pieced quilt top, Mosaic Star, New York State, 1840–1845. 102″ x 100″. The star motifs are made of small hexagons. (America Hurrah Antiques)

38 (opposite, below left). Pieced quilt, Blazing Star, Michigan, c. 1870. 79″ x 66″. The blazing star central motif was stitched from countless fabric diamonds. The double and triple borders are in the Sawtooth pattern. (Timothy and Pamela Hill)

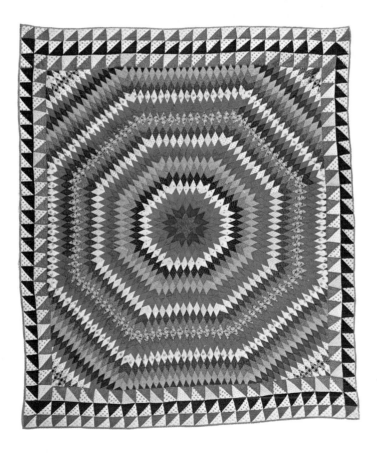

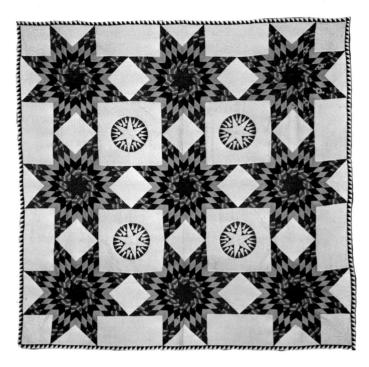

39 (above). Pieced quilt, Ship's Wheel, New England, c. 1850. 114″ x 112″. The striped blue patches give a strong sense of spiraling motion to the stars. (America Hurrah Antiques)

40 (below). Pieced quilt, Sunburst, Pennsylvania, c. 1870. 81¾″ x 80½″. The many variants of the Sunburst and Star of Bethlehem designs were tremendously popular with nineteenth-century quilters. (Phyllis Haders)

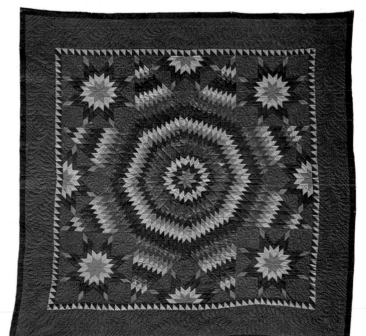

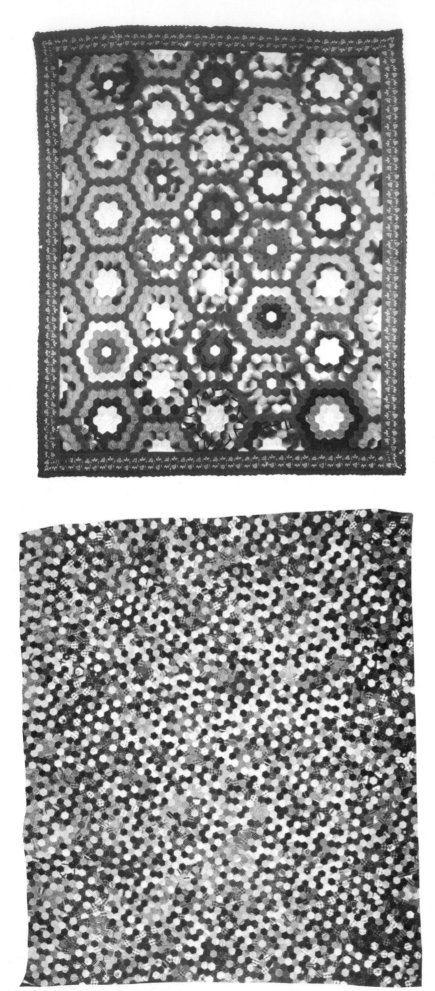

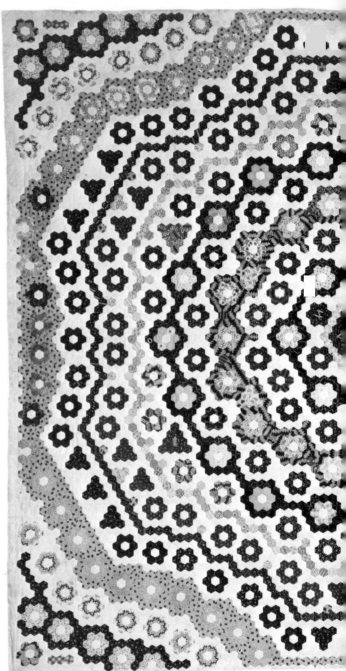

41 (left). Pieced quilt made by Amelia Emelina Wilson, Grandmother's Flower Garden, late nineteenth century. 91″ x 78″. A delicate, embroidered design of grapes and vines forms the border. (Cincinnati Art Museum; Gift of Mrs. J. Arthur Buhr)

42 (left). Pieced quilt top, Mosaic pattern, c. 1830. 75″ x 63″. This quilt top, constructed of silk hexagons, is also known as the Honeycomb Quilt, for it resembles the waxen cells made for storage by the honey bees. (Baltimore County Historical Society Museum)

44 (right). Pieced quilt top, Mosaic Star, Pennsylvania, nineteenth century. 100″ x 90¼″. (Allan Smith)

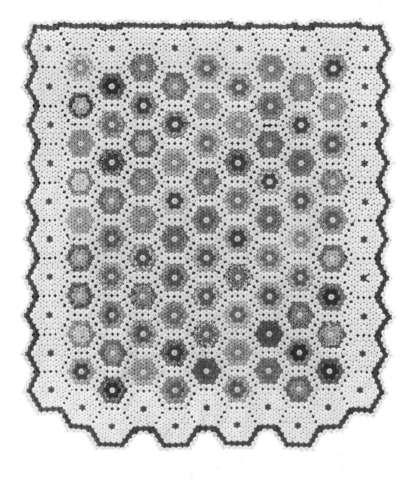

45 (below). Pieced quilt, Mosaic Star, silk, Philadelphia, c. 1865. 83¾″ x 77½″. (Phyllis Haders)

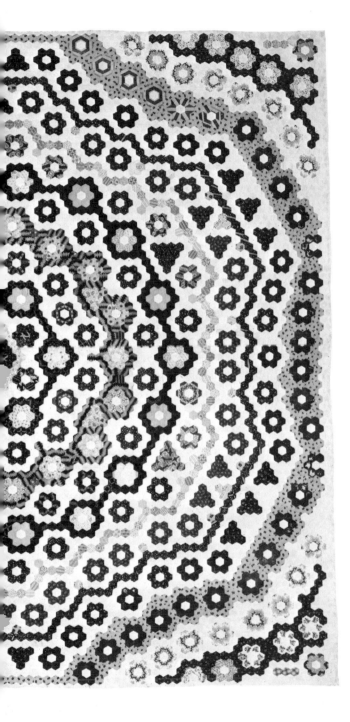

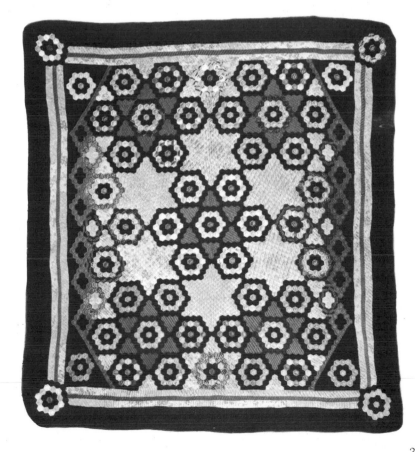

43 (center). Pieced quilt, Mosaic, c. 1840. 126″ x 120″. This enormous spread is a wonderfully complex and flowing design made of early cottons. (George E. Schoellkopf Gallery)

37

47 (right). Pieced quilt, Cobweb, Pennsylvania, c. 1900. 86″ x 86″. The color and organization of the elements in this quilt speak for themselves. (America Hurrah Antiques)

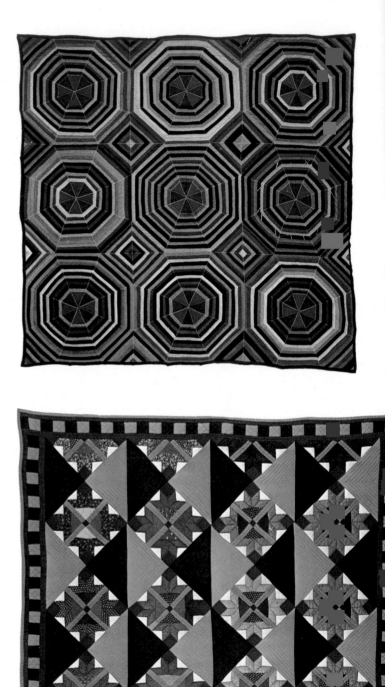

46 (below). Pieced quilt, Philadelphia Pavement, Pennsylvania, c. 1890. 85¼″ x 84¼″. This dazzling display of needlework was created by a true artist. (Thos. K. Woodard: American Antiques & Quilts)

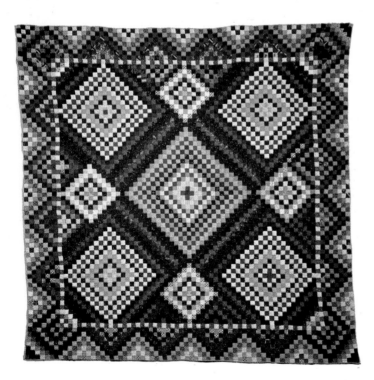

48 (right). Pieced quilt, Cross and Crown, Pennsylvania, c. 1860. 84″ x 72″. Texture, shape, and color combine here to form an exciting graphic design. (Timothy and Pamela Hill)

49 (left). Pieced Mennonite quilt, Geometric Star, made by Amy Bucher, Lebanon County, Pennsylvania, c. 1889. 83¾" x 79¾". Before making this quilt, Miss Bucher had already made two Star of Bethlehem quilts on red backgrounds. She used the scraps from those projects to make this brilliant example of the quilter's art. (Thos. K. Woodard: American Antiques & Quilts)

50 (below, left). Pieced quilt, Crossword Puzzle Squares, c. 1850. Variable Stars are set into the strips dividing the squares. (Rhea Goodman: Quilt Gallery, Inc.)

51 (below). Pieced quilt, Grandmother's Dream, Pennsylvania, c. 1920. 95¼" x 91½". (Kelter-Malcé Antiques)

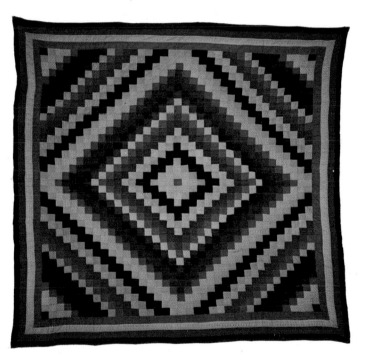

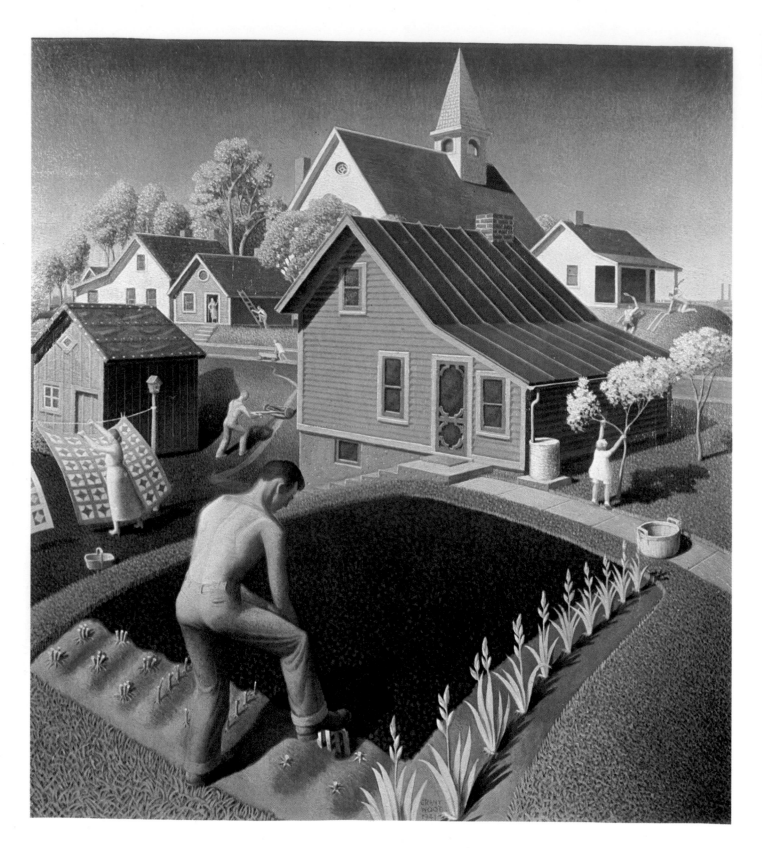

52 (above). *Spring in Town* by Grant Wood. Oil on panel. 1941.
26¼″ x 24½″. Grant Wood is best known for his haunting portrayals
of American rural life. A woman is seen hanging a pieced quilt on the
line to dry. (Sheldon Swope Art Gallery)

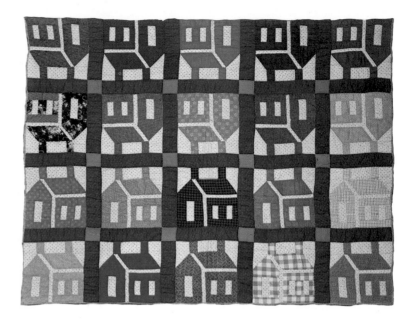

53 (right). Pieced quilt, Schoolhouse, c. 1895.
(America Hurrah Antiques)

54 (below). Pieced quilt, Schoolhouse in a Garden
Maze, Ohio, 1890–1895. (America Hurrah Antiques)

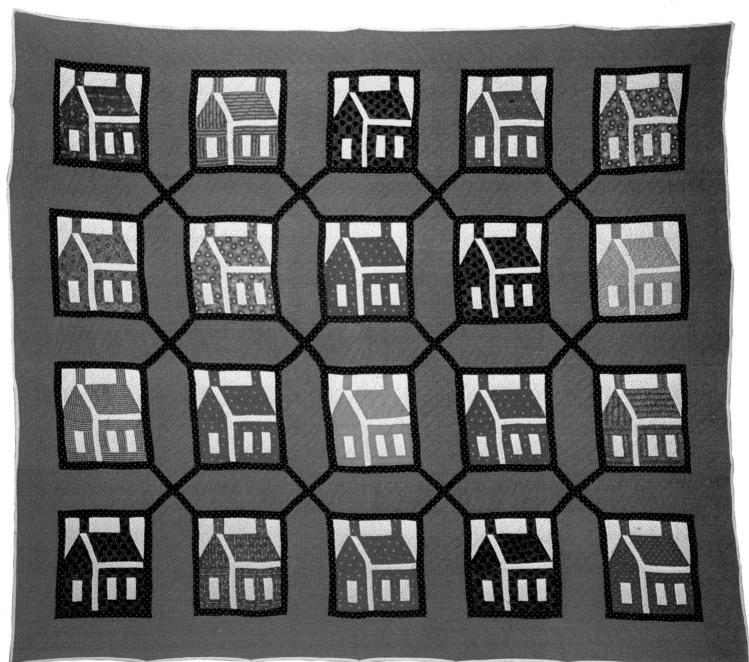

55 (below). Pieced quilt, Variable Star with Sawtooth border, c. 1840. 101″ x 88″. The blue-and-yellow fabric of the background is French. (The Pink House)

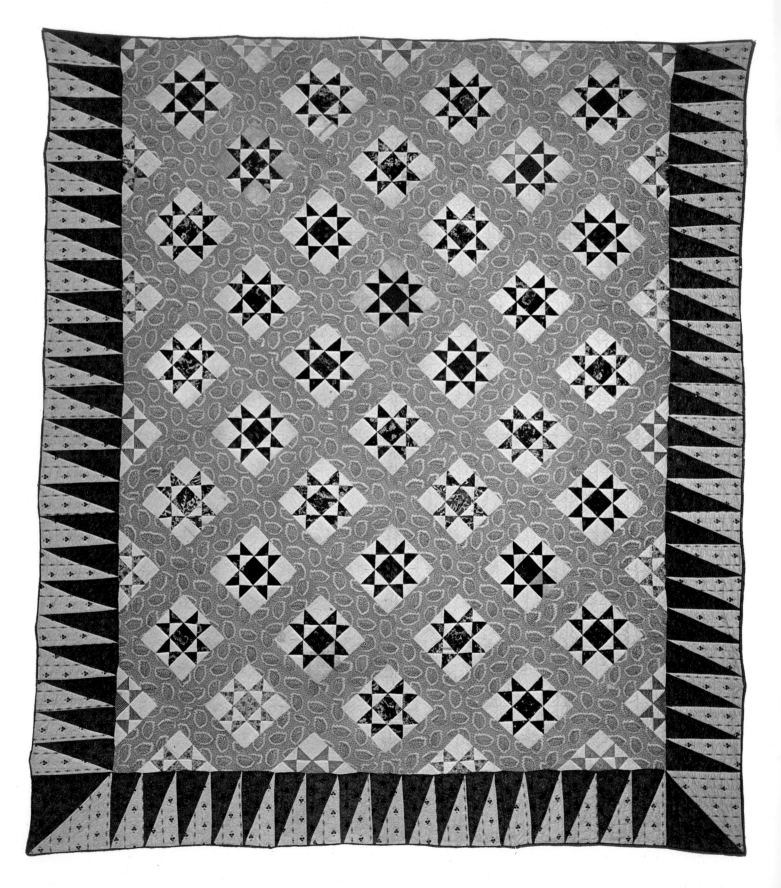

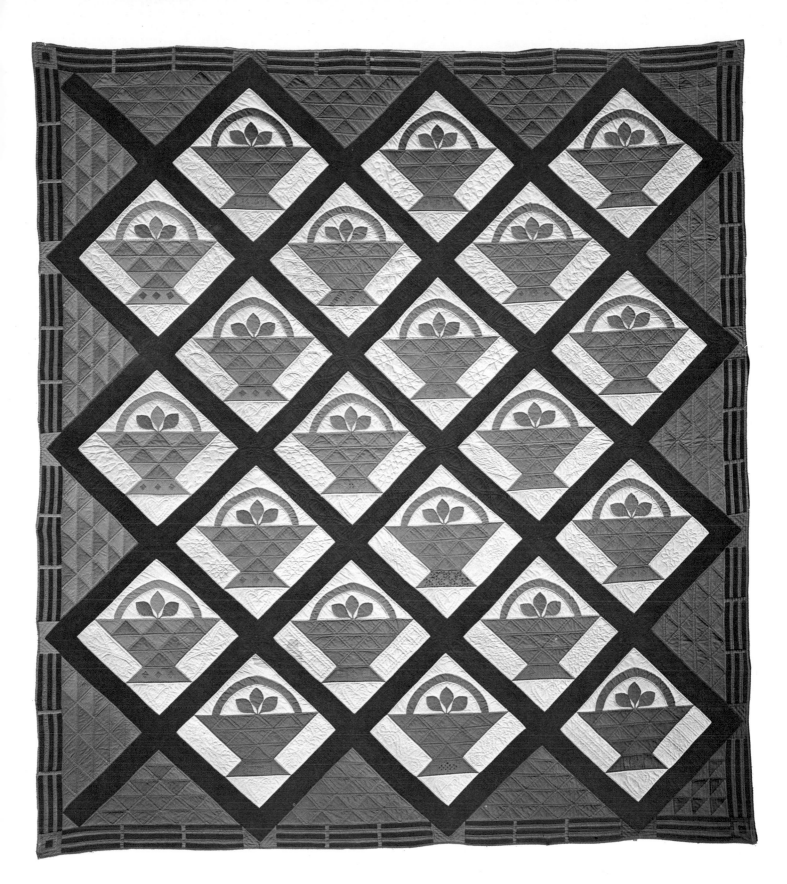

56 (above). Pieced quilt, Flower Basket, New Jersey, 1855. 95¾″ x 84¾″. Initialed MG and TMR. This beautifully designed and boldly colorful quilt has a quilted heart under each of the baskets. (Mrs. Samuel Schwartz)

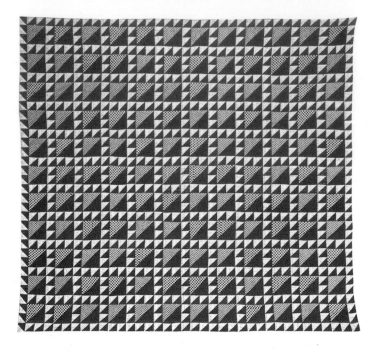

57 (above). Pieced quilt, Lady of the Lake, Pennsylvania, c. 1870. 98" x 92". Note how the plain and figured fabrics are effectively played against each other. (America Hurrah Antiques)

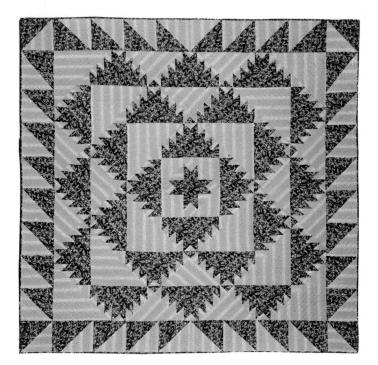

58 (above). Pieced quilt, Delectable Mountains, c. 1840. 88" x 84". Inscribed "Caroline Randall 12." (America Hurrah Antiques)

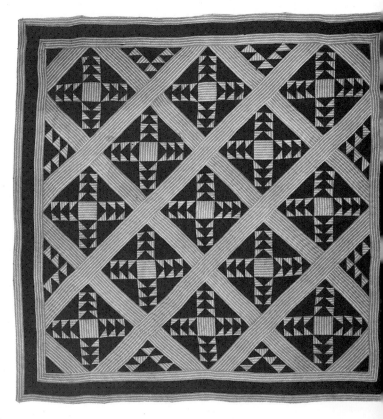

59 (above). Pieced quilt, Sawtooth, Indiana, c. 1885. 79" x 71". (Mr. and Mrs. Henry J. Rutkowski)

60 (below). Pieced quilt, Wild Goose Chase, Pennsylvania, c. 1860. The shades of red and green in this quilt are unusual. (Betty Sterling)

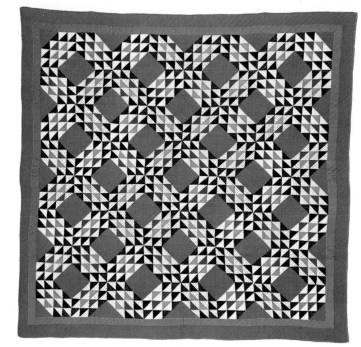

61 (right). Pieced quilt, Ocean Waves, Indiana, c. 1890.
80" x 80". (Patricia and James Rutkowski)

62 (below). Pieced quilt, Lady of the Lake, c. 1865.
85¾" x 70½". Note how the placement of the red and green
fabrics seems to create the motion of a pinwheel.
(America Hurrah Antiques)

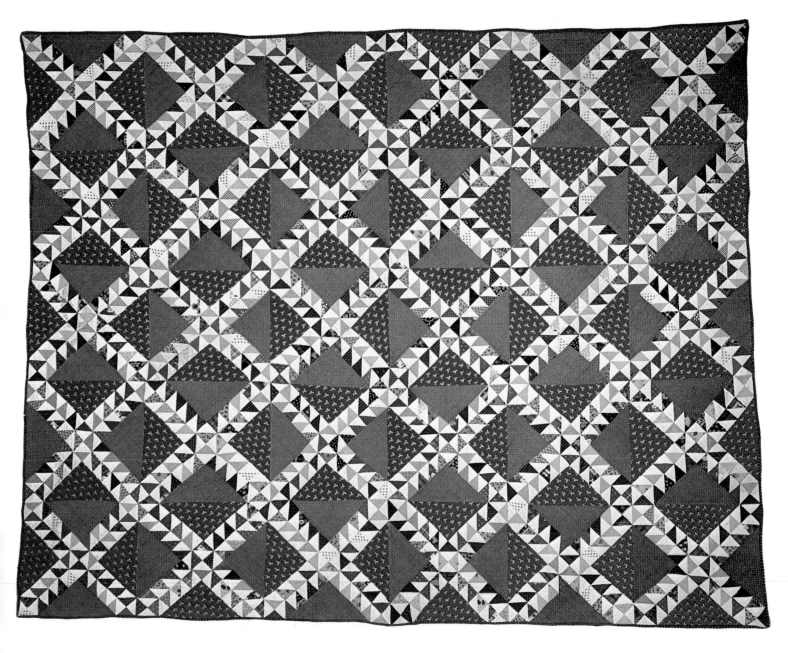

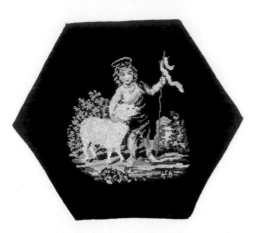

63 (below), and 63a (left). Pieced quilt, Baby's Blocks with Star, c. 1890. 66″ x 63¾″. This highly unusual piece has petit point designs incorporated into the star pattern. The quilting on the Baby's Blocks follows the outline of the patch, and all the points of the star are quilted in an ornate leaflike design. (The Pilgrim's Progress)

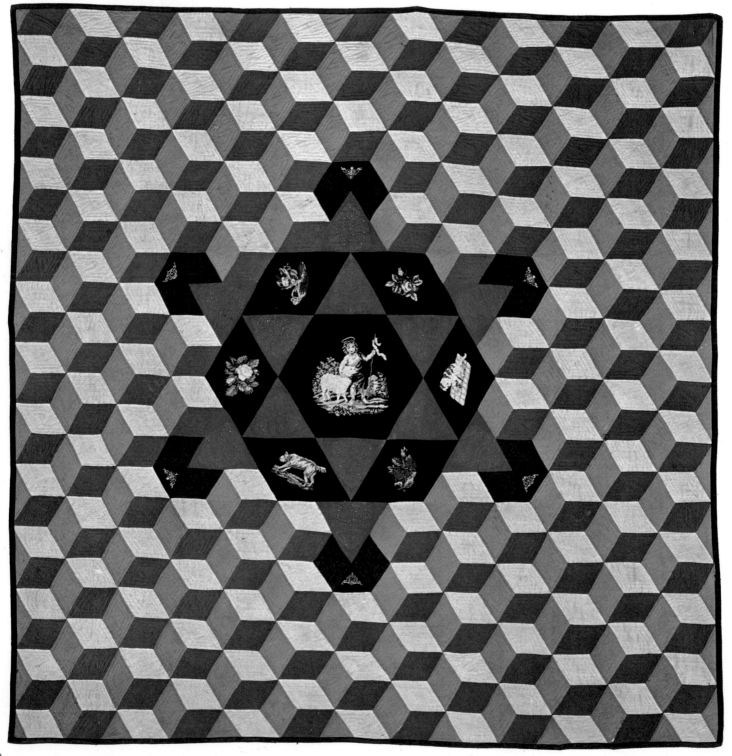

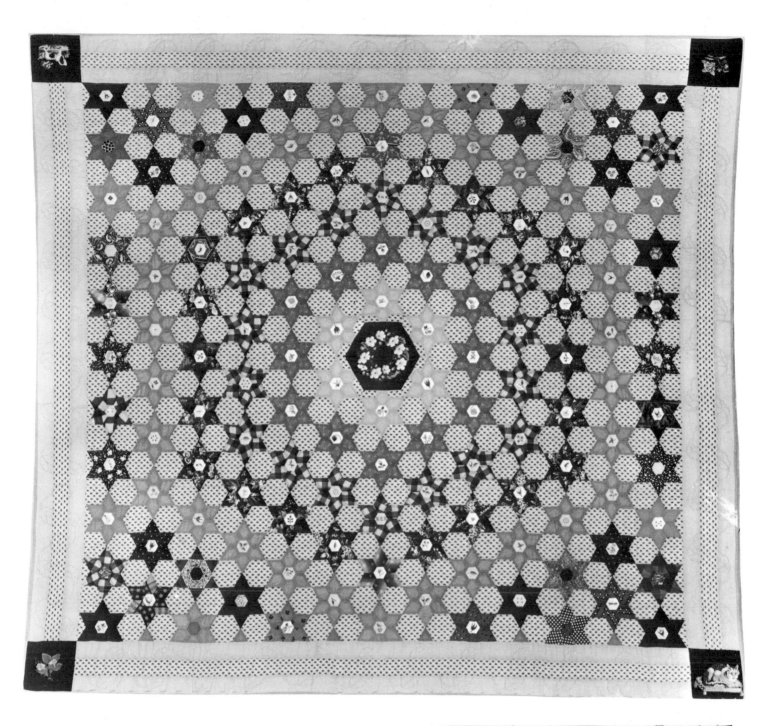

64 (above), 64a (right). Pieced quilt, Mosaic Star, Paris, Bourbon County, Kentucky, early 1860s. 75" x 79½". This quilt was made for Elinor Branham by her sisters. The central motif is a woolen floral wreath, and the centers of most of the stars have an embroidered leaf or flower. At two corners are flowers and at the other two a cat and a dog, worked in petit point. (Molly Davis)

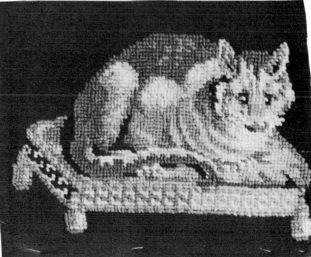

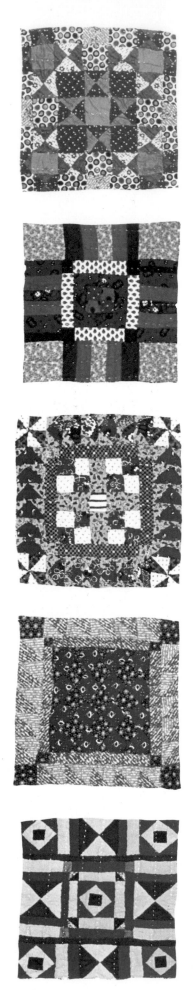

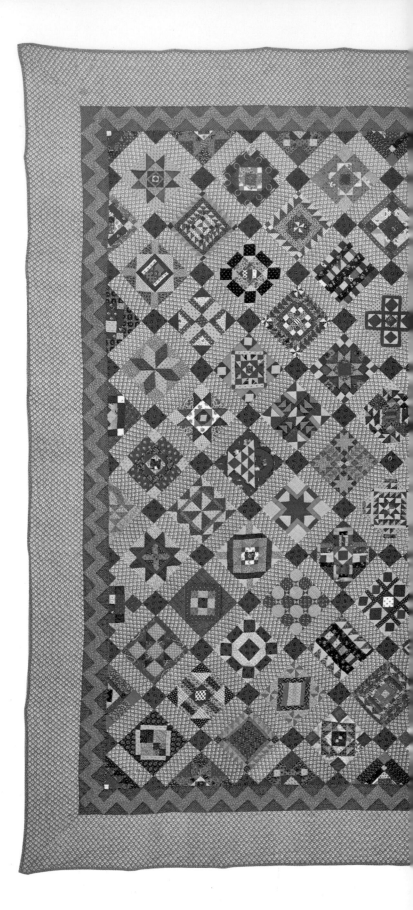

65 (above, and details at left and right). Pieced quilt, Sampler, Lancaster County, Pennsylvania, c. 1870. 88″ x 87¾″. This unique bedcover is one of the most fascinating American quilts known. It bears the stenciled inscription "Salinda W. Rupp." The maker had every right to be proud of her

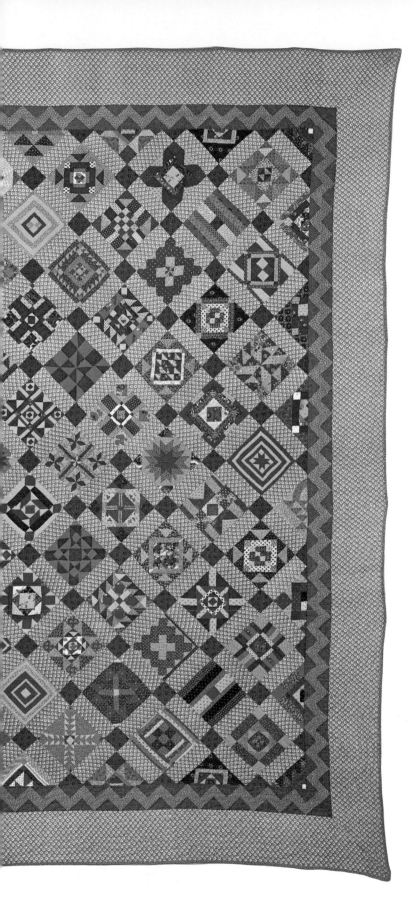

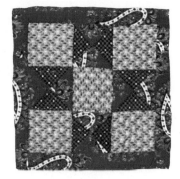

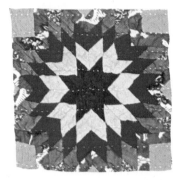

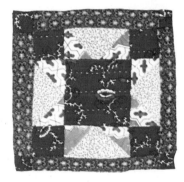

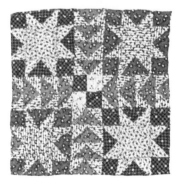

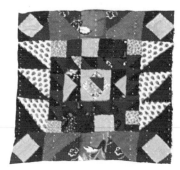

creation, for each colorful pieced block testifies to her
artistry. Each of the blocks is different from the others; some
are based on such familiar patterns as Variable Star, Sunburst,
and Flower Basket, but others are obviously Miss Rupp's
original creations. (America Hurrah Antiques)

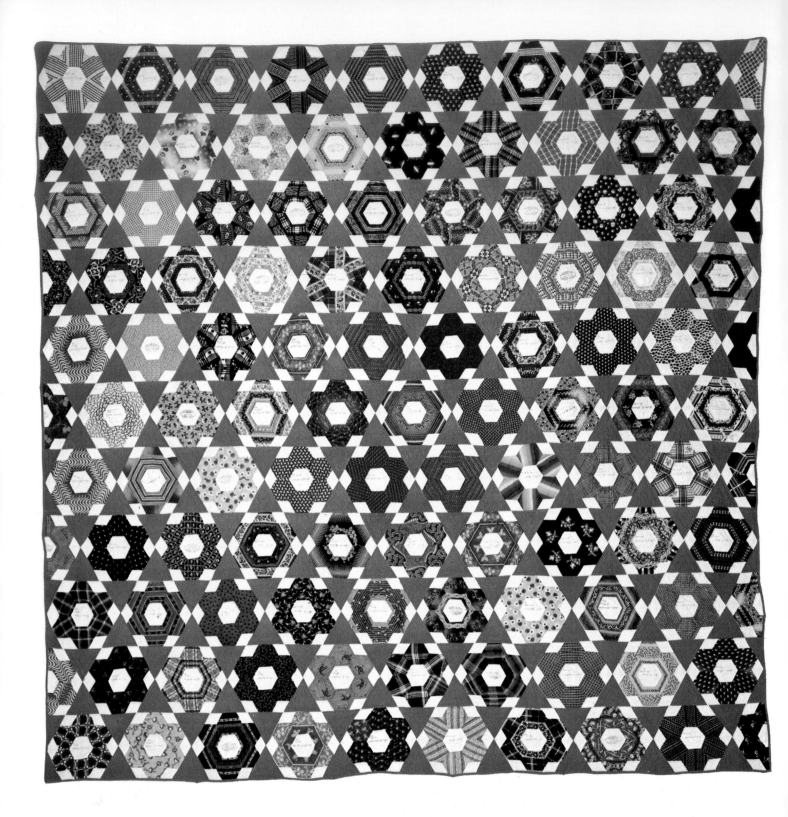

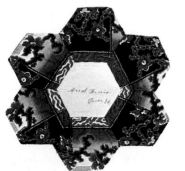

66 (above, and details, below). Pieced Friendship quilt, Mosaic Star, New Hampshire, c. 1845. 84″ x 84″. The patchwork center of every star is signed or stamped with the name of its maker. The individual blocks were worked by many women and finally assembled into a gift that would be treasured by its recipient. Note especially the wealth of handsome mid-nineteenth-century fabrics used. (America Hurrah Antiques)

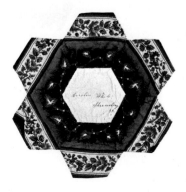

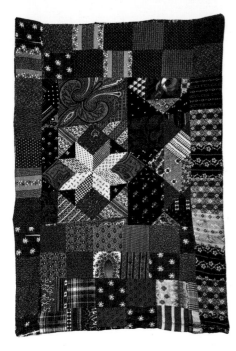

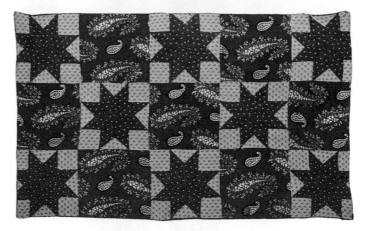

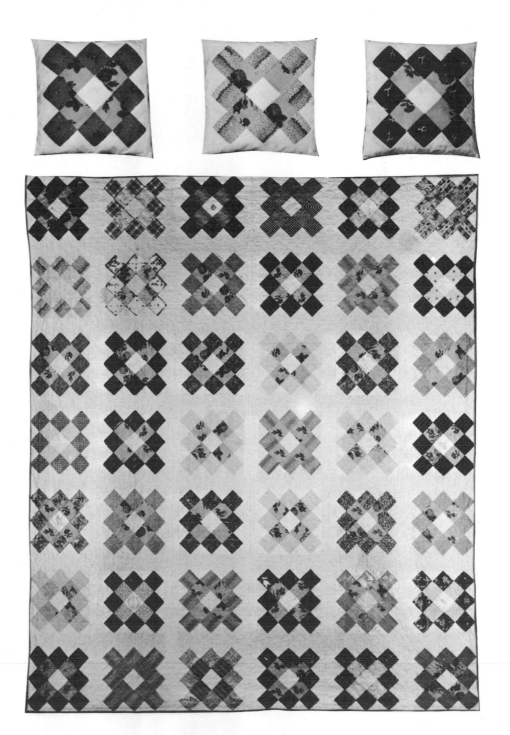

67 (above, left). Pieced pillowcase, Pennsylvania, c. 1880. 24½″ x 16½″. The center section of this case is printed to look like patchwork, and the surrounding border has been pieced. (America Hurrah Antiques)

68 (above, right). Pieced pillowcase, Variable Star, Pennsylvania, c. 1860. 26½″ x 16¾″. The design of pillowcases sometimes matched the design of the quilt, much like those illustrated in figure 69. (America Hurrah Antiques)

69 (right). Pieced quilt, Friendship or Autograph, with three matching pillowcases, Midwest, c. 1844. 88″ x 77″. (Cincinnati Art Museum; Gift of John A. C. March)

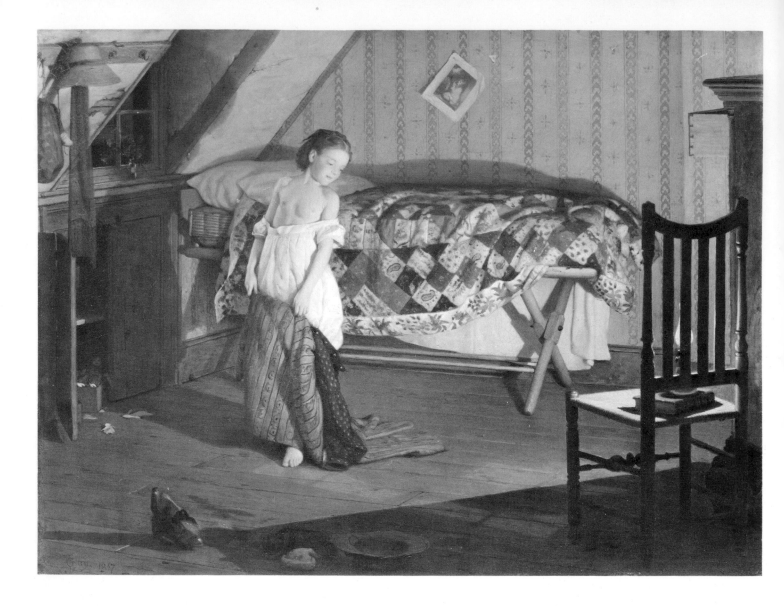

70 (above). *Making a Train* by Seymour Joseph Guy, 1867.
Oil on canvas. 24⅜″ x 18⅛″. How beautifully this painting
of an attic room captures the essence of a young girl's fantasy
of grown-up elegance! Her bedding with its pieced quilt
rests on a cot, and the banister-back chair at the right is an
old-fashioned survivor from the mid-eighteenth century,
relegated to the attic. (Philadelphia Museum of Art;
George W. Elkins Collection)

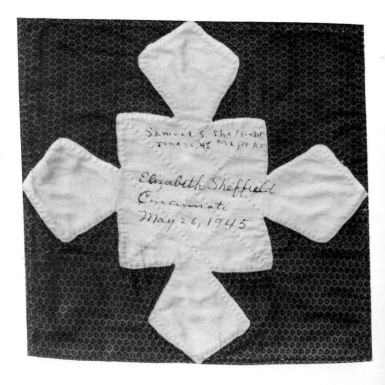

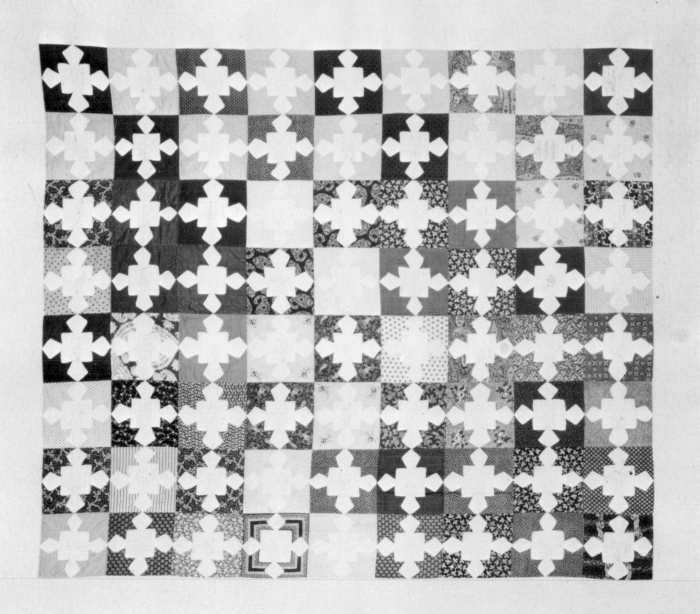

The tender tie of friendship binds
Our hearts in mutual love

Miss Lucy A. Smith
Warren Oct 1852
R. J.

71 (below), 71a (left), 71b (opposite, below). Pieced and appliqué Autograph quilt. This rare piece was begun by Mary Caroline Wooley Smith of Cincinnati, Ohio, in 1840, and finished by her granddaughter, Mrs. Russell Wilson, in 1950. 94″ x 87½″. Many of the signed patches are from the 1840 period and were made by friends from Cincinnati and nearby Lexington, Kentucky. The final quilting was executed at the Cincinnati Women's Exchange. The appliqués are signed with both stamped and handwritten signatures. Some have been further embellished with sentimental phrases. (Cincinnati Art Museum; Gift of Mrs. Russell Wilson)

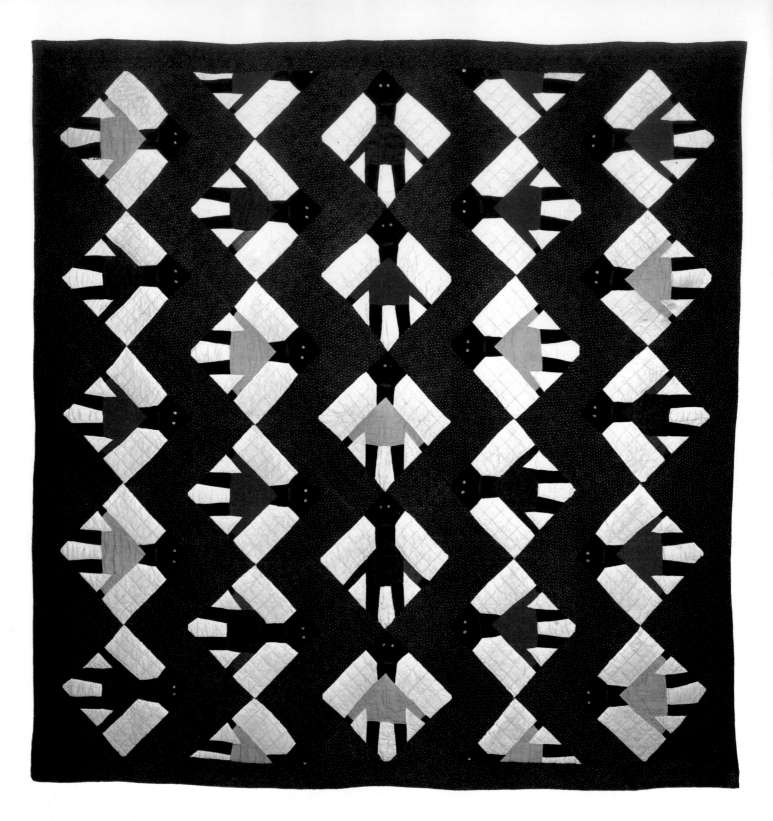

72 (above), 72a (opposite, above). Pieced quilt, southern Missouri, c. 1900. 73½″ x 71″. Basically, this extraordinary quilt is in the Streak o' Lightning pattern, but it has been made a very exciting graphic statement by the addition of the strong black figures with embroidered mouths and eyes. (America Hurrah Antiques)

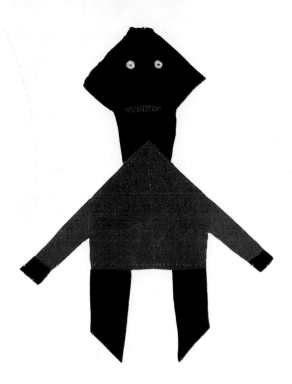

73 (below). Pieced quilt top, c. 1890. 64" x 82". The maker of this piece succeeded in giving it a strong three-dimensional quality. Her strategic use of one band of a darker blue material imparts extra interest to the whole. (Private collection; photograph courtesy America Hurrah Antiques)

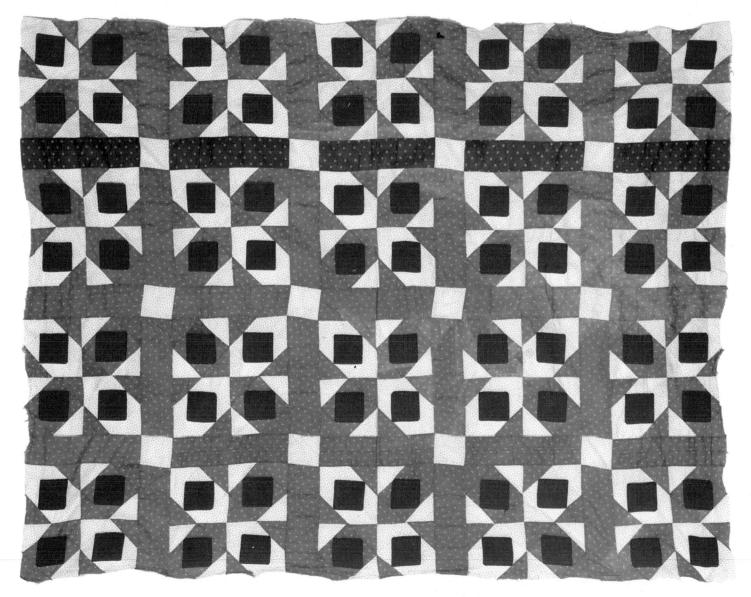

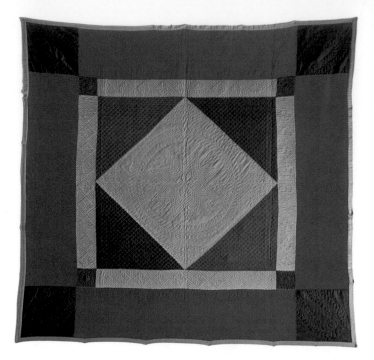

74 (below). Pieced quilt, Bars, Amish, Pennsylvania, c. 1900. 80″ x 76″. (Private collection; photograph courtesy George E. Schoellkopf Gallery)

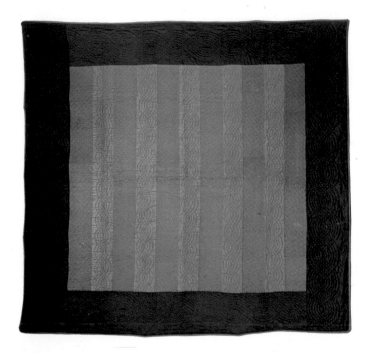

75 (below). Pieced quilt, Bars, Amish, Pennsylvania, c. 1900. 78″ x 78″. Note the fine basket and feather quilting. (Private collection; photograph courtesy George E. Schoellkopf Gallery)

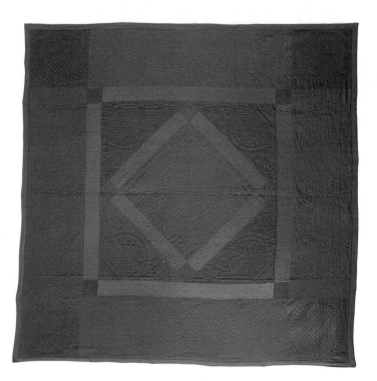

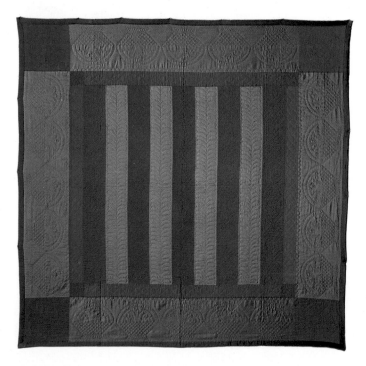

76 (top). Pieced quilt, Diamond in Square, Amish, Pennsylvania, c. 1920. 78″ x 75¾″. The quilting in this piece is especially elaborate, with a large Variable Star featured in the center diamond.

77 (above). Pieced quilt, Diamond in Square, Amish, Lancaster County, Pennsylvania, c. 1915. 78″ x 77″. The striking colors work splendidly together in this piece. Note the scrolled feather quilting in the brown border. (Phyllis Haders)

78 (opposite). Pieced quilt, Amish, Pennsylvania, initialed AK and dated 1892. The dating of this piece is a rarity, and the rich colors are particularly handsome. (George E. Schoellkopf Gallery)

AMISH QUILTS

Amish settlers from Switzerland and Germany established themselves in Pennsylvania near the beginning of the eighteenth century. This sect, a segment of the Mennonite church, was founded in 1693 by Jacob Amman, a Swiss. Their religious tenets prescribe that the Amish live strictly by the Bible and close to the land.

The simplicity of this life-style even extends to their unusually handsome quilts, which are generally fashioned of plain fabrics in both bright and somber colors and stitched together in geometric patterns.

The strong, bold designs and unusual palette of most Amish quilts have a particular appeal to modern taste. Consequently, fine Amish quilts are much sought after and prized by collectors.

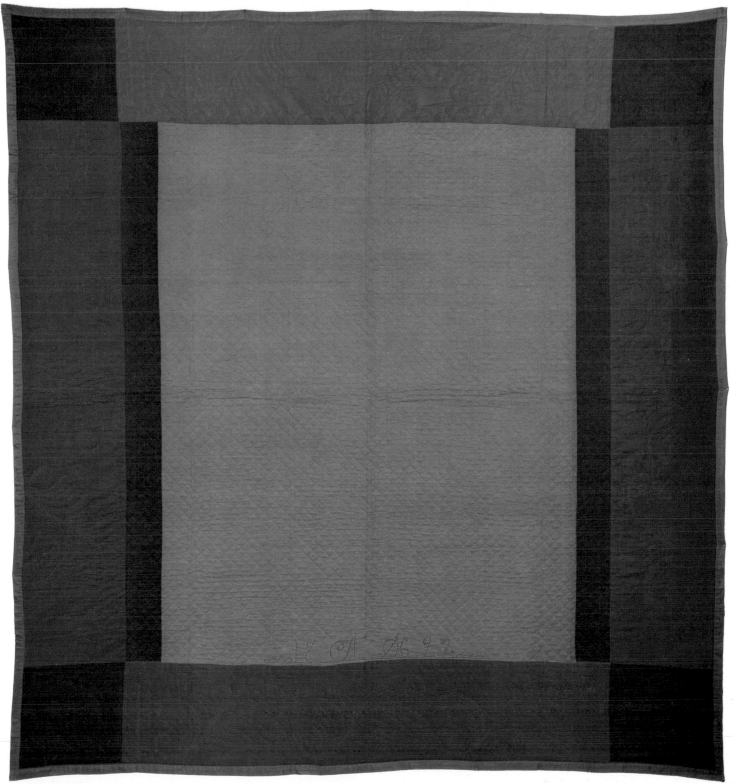

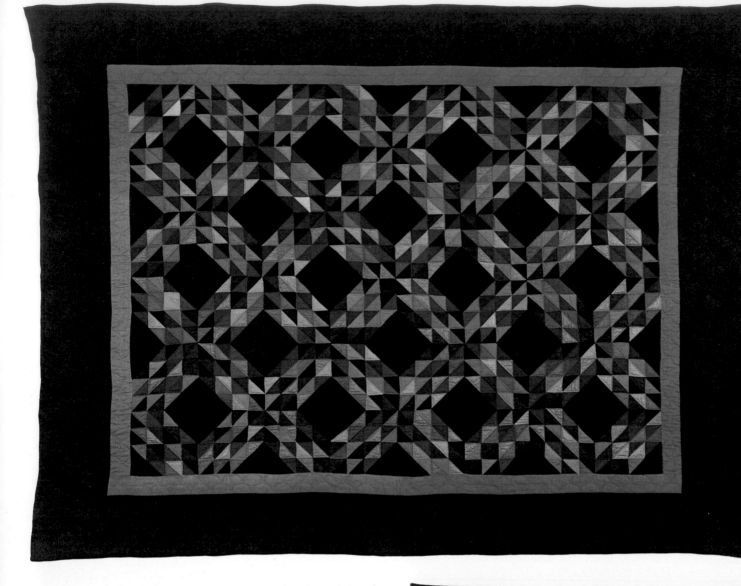

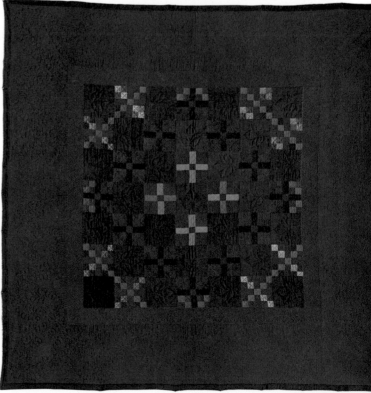

79 (above). Pieced quilt, Ocean Waves, Amish, Ohio, c. 1915. 66″ x 85″. Both the Amish and Mennonites are called "plain people," but the Mennonites are for the most part less conservative than the Amish. (Patricia and James Rutkowski)

80 (right). Pieced quilt, Amish, Lancaster County, Pennsylvania, 1910–1920. 83½″ x 83″. Made of wool, this quilt is notable both for the richness of the colors and for the way they have been arranged in the central design. (Lois Stulberg; photograph courtesy Adirondack Memories)

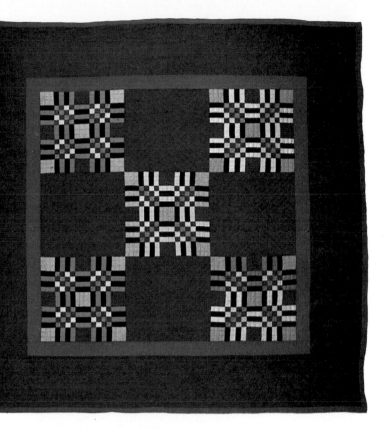

81 (left). Pieced quilt, Amish, Pennsylvania, 1890–1900. 82″ x 81″. This is a most unusual design to find in an Amish quilt. A successful sewing machine was patented in 1846 by Elias Howe, Jr. Even after this timesaving device had become common to American households, most quilts continued to be made by hand. *Godey's Lady's Book*, the housewife's bible in all matters of taste and culture, made the following observation in an article on "Mosaic Patchwork" in the May, 1883, issue: "It saves time if a few of the smaller pieces are joined by a sewing machine, but we would suggest only a little of this being done as it gives straight lines." (Mr. and Mrs. Edwin Braman)

82 (below). Pieced quilt, Ocean Waves, Amish, Tuscarawas County, Ohio, 1880–1890. 79″ x 60½″. Henry Davis of Chicago invented a quilting attachment for sewing machines in 1892. This ingenious affair enabled a woman to quilt "comforts, quilts, coat linings, dress skirts, and any other article which it is desired to have filled with cotton or wool."[14] Most quilters have fortunately scorned such mechanical devices. (Phyllis Haders)

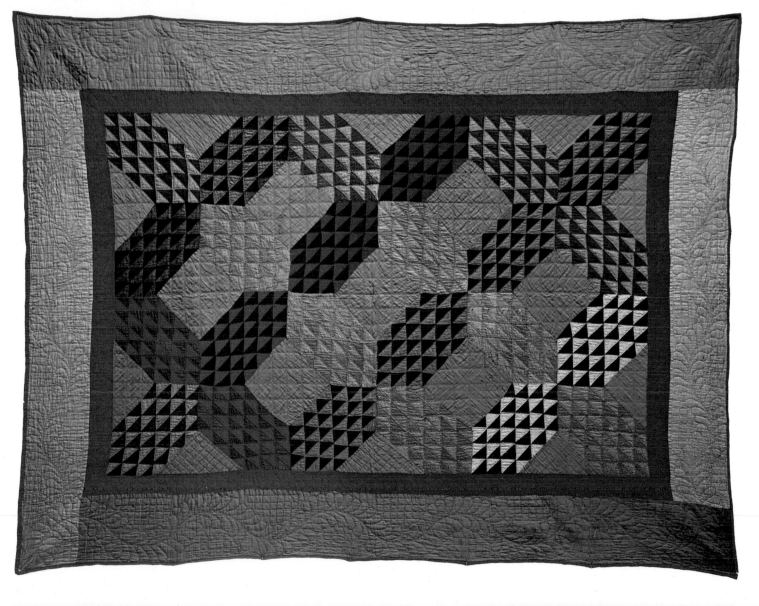

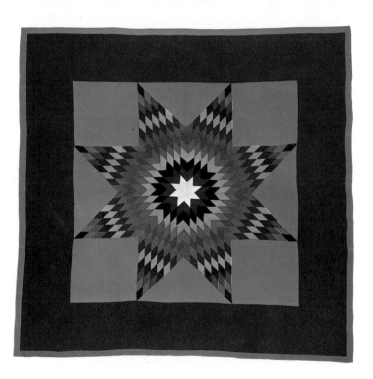

83 (below). Pieced quilt, variously known as Grandmother's Dream, Sunshine and Shadow, or Trip Around the World, Amish, Pennsylvania, c. 1900. The colors in this piece are particularly brilliant, and the Sawtooth border is unusual. (George E. Schoellkopf Gallery)

84 (right). Pieced quilt, Jacob's Ladder, Amish, Pennsylvania, c. 1900. 86" x 77". (George E. Schoellkopf Gallery)

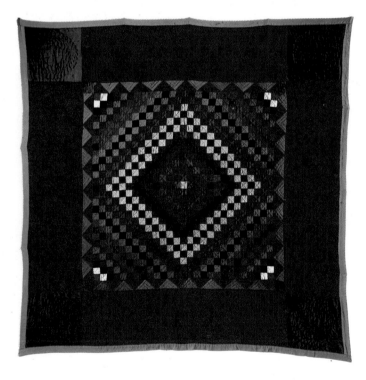

85 (above). Pieced quilt, Star of Bethlehem, Amish, Pennsylvania, c. 1925. 88" x 86". Mennonite quilts tend to be more complex than those made by Amish women. The Mennonites' use of printed cottons in their quilts was often criticized by the Amish. (Patricia and James Rutkowski)

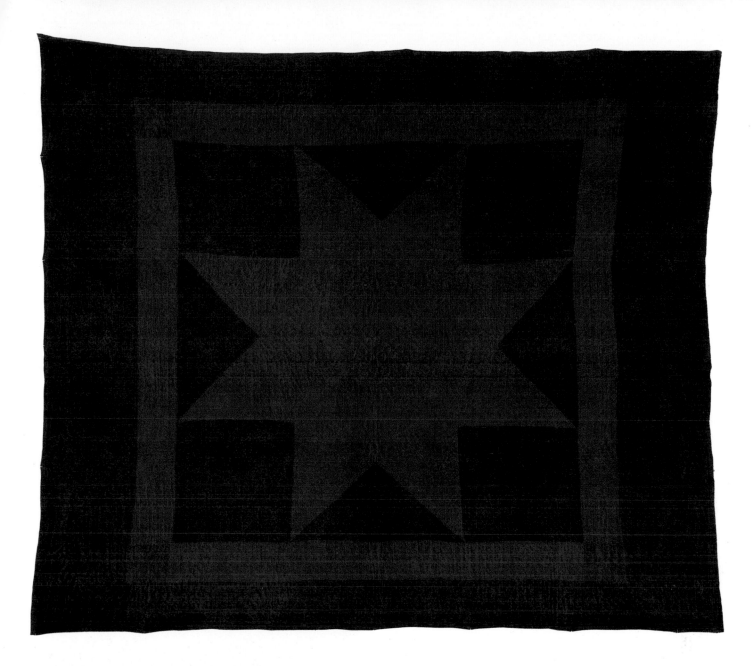

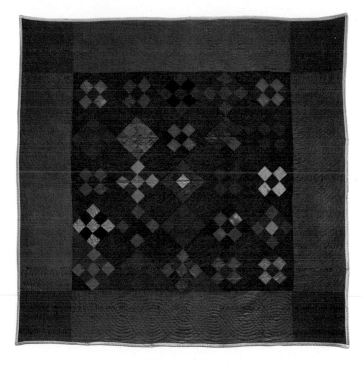

86 (above). Pieced quilt, Lone Star, Amish, made by Susan H. Hochstettler, Lancaster County, Pennsylvania, c. 1848. 74″ x 86″. The color, design, and quilting all combine to make this a superlative piece. Susan Hochstettler, whose family came to America in 1736 from Switzerland, was born in Somerset County, Pennsylvania, in 1826 and died in 1897. (Phyllis Haders)

87 (left). Pieced quilt, Nine Patch, Amish, Lancaster County, Pennsylvania, c. 1890. 82″ x 80″. Like a great many Amish quilts, this bedcover is worked in wool. (Phyllis Haders)

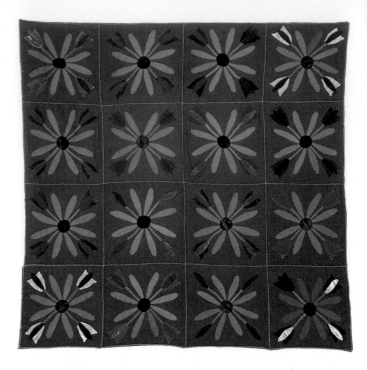

89 (right). Appliqué quilt, Amish, Lancaster County, Pennsylvania, c. 1895. Appliqué quilts made by the Amish are most unusual. The tulip blossoms in this quilt have been cut from velvet, which may well represent an intrusion of Victorian taste into the culture of the "plain people." (Phyllis Haders)

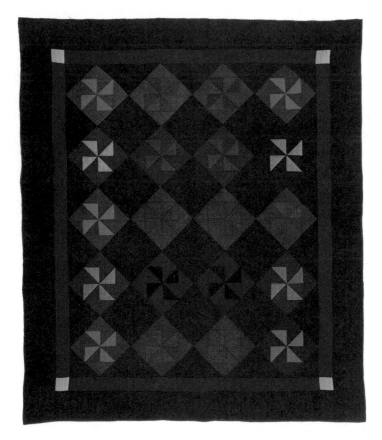

88 (above). Pieced quilt, Pinwheel, Amish, Indiana, c. 1890. 82″ x 69″. Most surviving Amish quilts date from after the mid-nineteenth century. (Patricia and James Rutkowski)

91 (right). Pieced quilt, Log Cabin, Windmill Blades design, Amish, Pennsylvania, c. 1900. 86¾" x 69¼". Tiny golden bugs have been embroidered in the centers of the purple-and-black "blades." (George E. Schoellkopf Gallery)

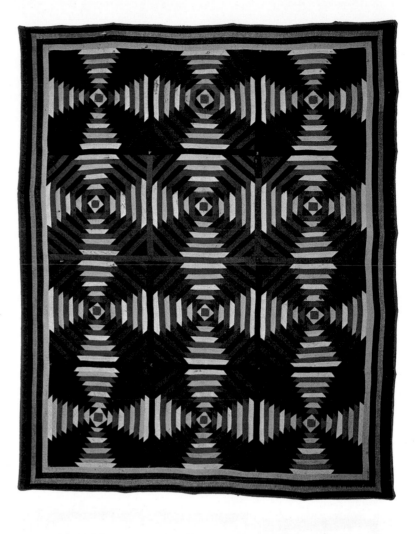

90 (center). Pieced quilt, Irish Chain, Amish, probably Home County, Ohio, c. 1910. 88½" x 70". Here again we find great color and great quilting masterfully combined. (Malcolm Kirk)

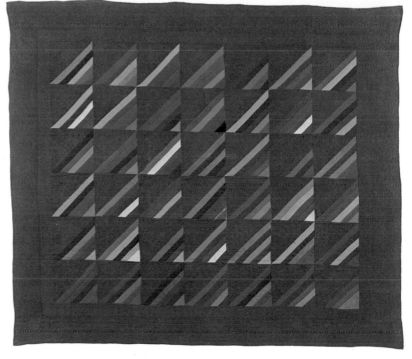

92 (above). Pieced quilt, Rainbow Block or Roman Stripes, Amish, Indiana, c. 1920. 68" x 80". The startling diagonal motion of the rainbow stripes is abruptly checked by the contrasting patches of plain brown wool. (Timothy and Pamela Hill)

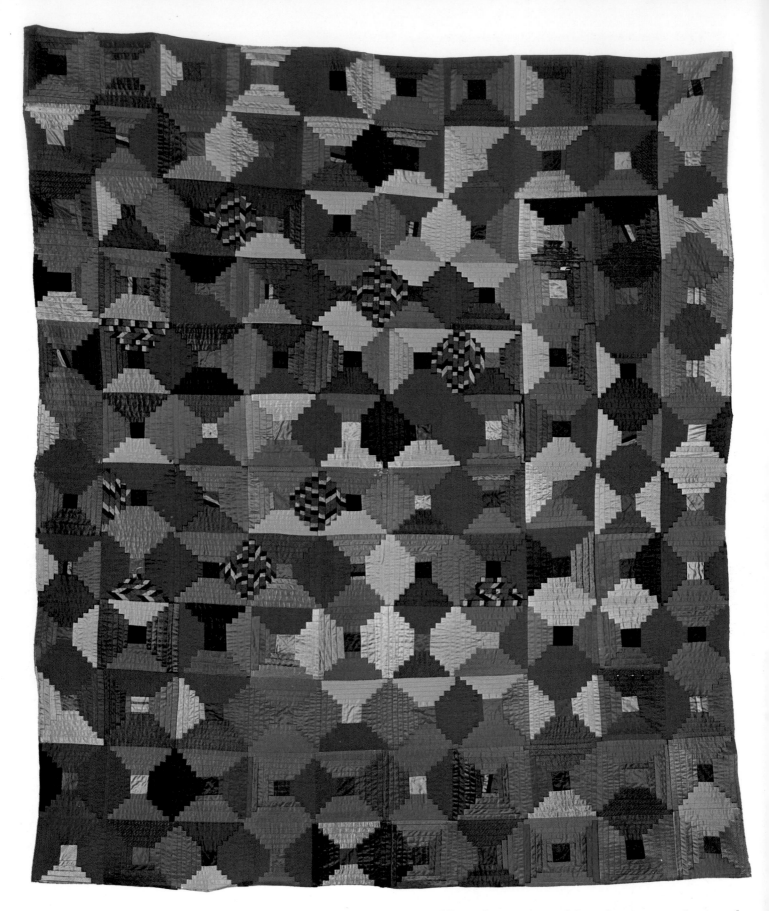

93 (above). Pieced quilt, Log Cabin, Courthouse Steps design, made by Samuel Steinberger, New York City, 1890–1900. 68" x 56". This quilt, which was probably used as a parlor throw, is not only sumptuous in color, but also of special interest because it is rare to find a quilt known to have been made by a man. Samuel Steinberger was a tailor, and his quilt is constructed from the remnants of satin and velvet he used to line vests and coats. While the quilt is based on the Courthouse Steps design, its maker chose to vary the blocks in many ways; so the result is quite abstract. (Private collection; photograph courtesy America Hurrah Antiques)

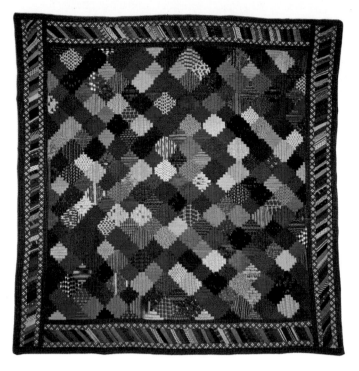

LOG CABIN QUILTS

Log Cabin quilts became popular by the mid-nineteenth century. Many types were made from narrow rectangles and small squares of fabric, and the results are particularly graphic examples of the quilter's art.

A Log Cabin quilt rarely had an inner lining and consequently was seldom quilted. If it was, the quilting often followed the lines of the "log" or individual piece. Ornate quilting usually appears only on open borders, for it would have been especially difficult to quilt a design over so many seams. The quilt top on most Log Cabin pieces is "tufted" or tied to the backing.

Boys used to be taught many forms of sewing. Some were even encouraged to assist in making a quilt. Calvin Coolidge pieced a Baby's Blocks quilt at the age of ten. Dwight D. Eisenhower and his brother helped their mother fashion a quilt. Mary Schenck Woolman, a progressive teacher during the early twentieth century, recommended sewing for all schoolboys: "In the first three or four years . . . it is well for the boys and the girls to be taught the same kinds of handwork. . . . Experience has proved that boys are greatly interested in sewing when it is connected with their pursuits . . ."[15]

94 (above). Pieced quilt, Log Cabin, Courthouse Steps design, Pennsylvania, 1860–1870. 80¾" x 78". Made from challis, a fabric that was originally manufactured from silk and worsted at Norwich, England, in 1832. The term means soft, and it derives from the Indian word *shalee*. Challis is usually printed in small floral patterns. This quilt is framed by handsome diagonal stripes edged with a red-and-white print. (Thos. K. Woodard: American Antiques & Quilts)

95 (below). Pieced quilt, Log Cabin, Light and Dark design, Pennsylvania, c. 1900. 69½" x 81". (George E. Schoellkopf Gallery)

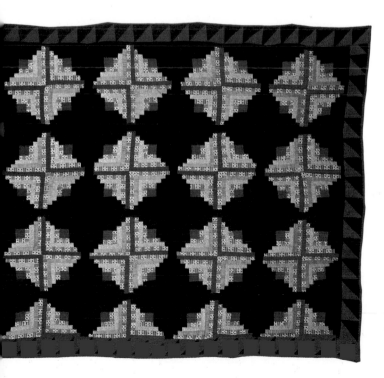

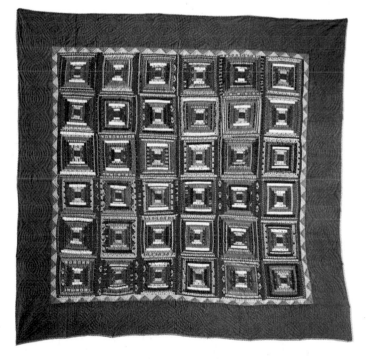

96 (above). Pieced quilt, Log Cabin, Courthouse Steps design, Pennsylvania, c. 1875. 86" x 84". The printed fabrics and colors in this quilt are especially attractive. (John and Mary Margaret Hansen; photograph courtesy America Hurrah Antiques)

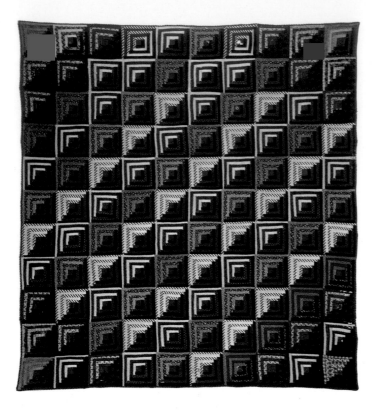

98 (below). Pieced quilt, Log Cabin, Straight Furrow design, silk taffeta, Pennsylvania, 1920s. 80″ x 75″. The white ties with which the quilt is tufted can be clearly seen in this illustration. (Kelter-Malcé Antiques)

97 (left). Pieced quilt, Log Cabin, Straight Furrow design, Pennsylvania, 1880–1885. 89″ x 81½″. Note how effectively the plain and patterned fabrics are used in the design. (Richard Miner)

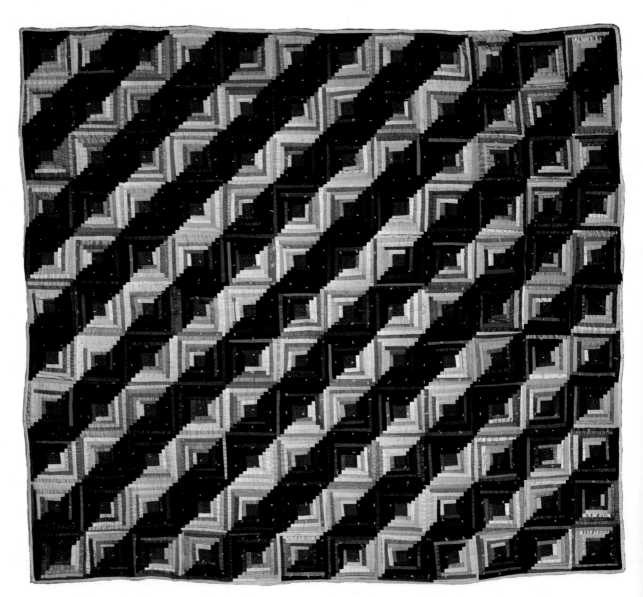

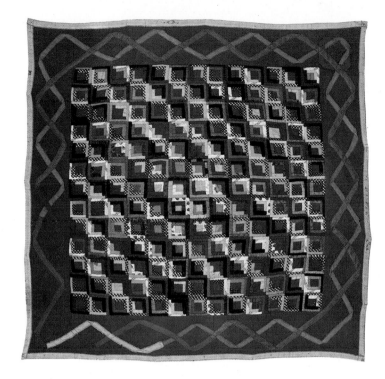

99 (left). Pieced crib quilt, Log Cabin, variation of the Straight Furrow design, Amish, Pennsylvania, c. 1865. 33¾″ x 33½″. Because of the diminutive size of this fascinating piece, it must have been very difficult to design and execute. The free-form border is particularly interesting. This Amish quilt is most unusual, for the "plain people" seldom allowed themselves the luxury of such a complex, intricate design. (America Hurrah Antiques)

100 (below). Pieced quilt, Log Cabin, Straight Furrow design, Pennsylvania, c. 1900. 66″ x 76″. The strong, dark colors make this a particularly handsome quilt. The four examples of the Straight Furrow pattern seen on these two pages give some idea of its graphic effectiveness. (America Hurrah Antiques)

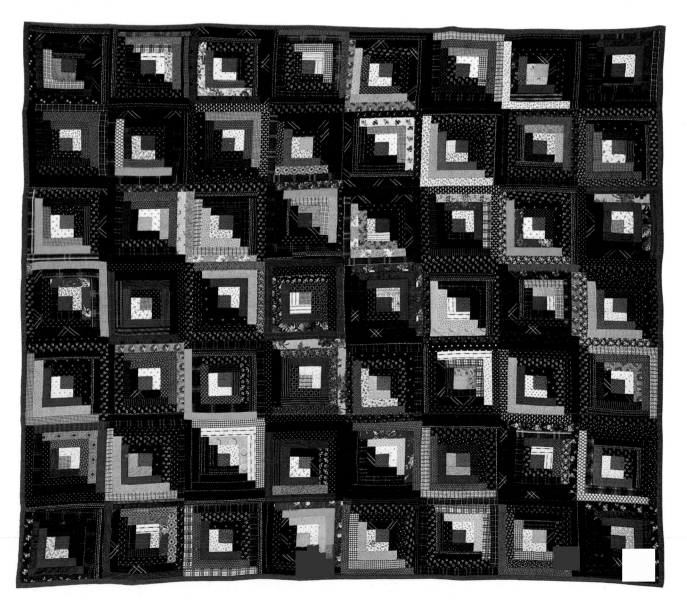

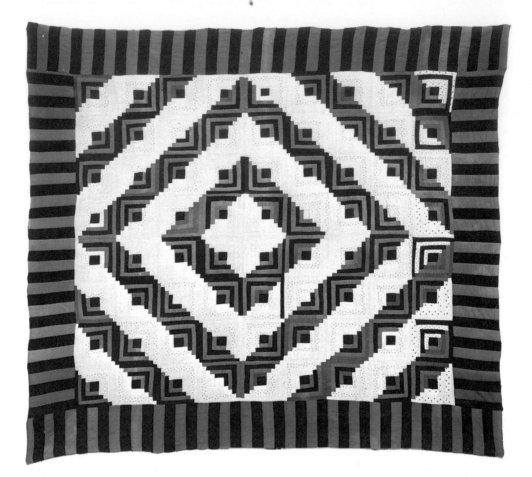

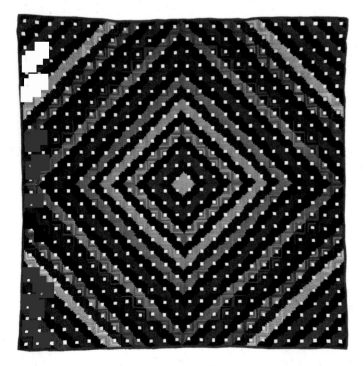

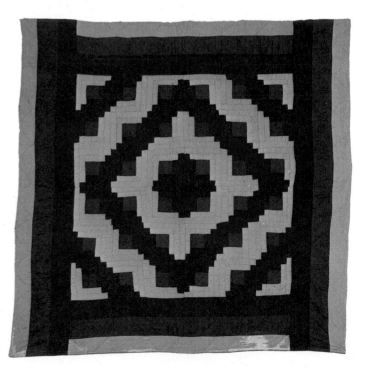

103 (below). Pieced crib quilt, Log Cabin, variation of Barn Raising design, Pennsylvania, 1885–1895. 39″ x 39″. This is good, strong Pennsylvania color to an unusual degree. (America Hurrah Antiques)

102 (above). Pieced quilt, Log Cabin, Barn Raising design, Pennsylvania, c. 1890. 81″ x 81″. The white "eyes" make a strong contribution to the graphic beauty of this quilt. (Bill Gallick and Tony Ellis)

101 (opposite, above). Pieced quilt top, Log Cabin, Barn Raising design, c. 1920. 68″ x 61½″. The particular fascination of this piece is realizing that its maker obviously decided she wasn't going to be bound by the rules of regular design. Notice how at the right of the quilt some of the red stripes or "logs" are placed in the white area and how an occasional red square is floated in the white. (Private collection; photograph courtesy Phyllis Haders)

104 (below). Pieced quilt, Log Cabin variation, New York State, 1880—1890. 71″ x 70″. Here is a country quilt at its best. The red strips and squares appear to be made of bandana material. (Kelter-Malcé Antiques)

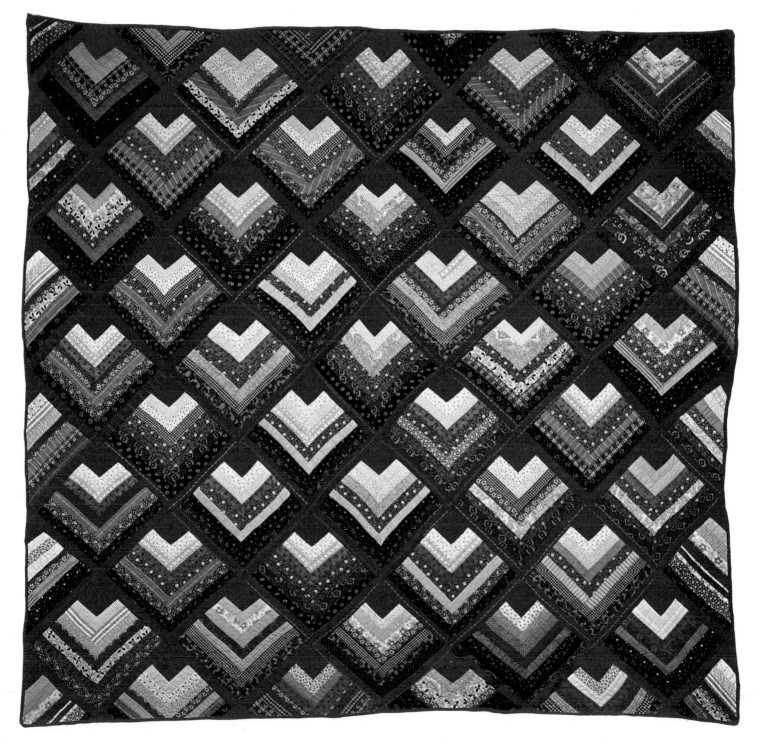

105 (below), 105a (right). Appliqué quilt, Friendship Album, Elizabeth Port, New Jersey, dated 1852. 99″ x 98″. This is a particularly beautiful and fascinating example of a presentation Friendship quilt. It was created by the Sewing Society of the Methodist Episcopal Church of Elizabeth Port and presented to a Mr. and Mrs. Dunn, who were missionaries and lay preachers to the South Pacific islands. It is probable that the actual Methodist Episcopal church building has been depicted in the third row from the top, and above the red Bible directly below the church is the inscription "God Is Love." Note the deer peering through the appliquéd branches in the bottom row. (Phyllis Haders)

106 (opposite, above). Appliqué quilt, Ohio, c. 1840. 96″ x 92″. The red-and-yellow elements of this rhythmically designed quilt are pineapples, the symbol of hospitality. See page 2 for an enlarged detail. (Timothy and Pamela Hill)

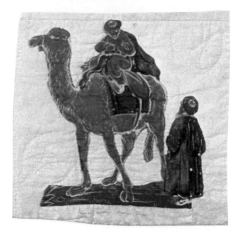

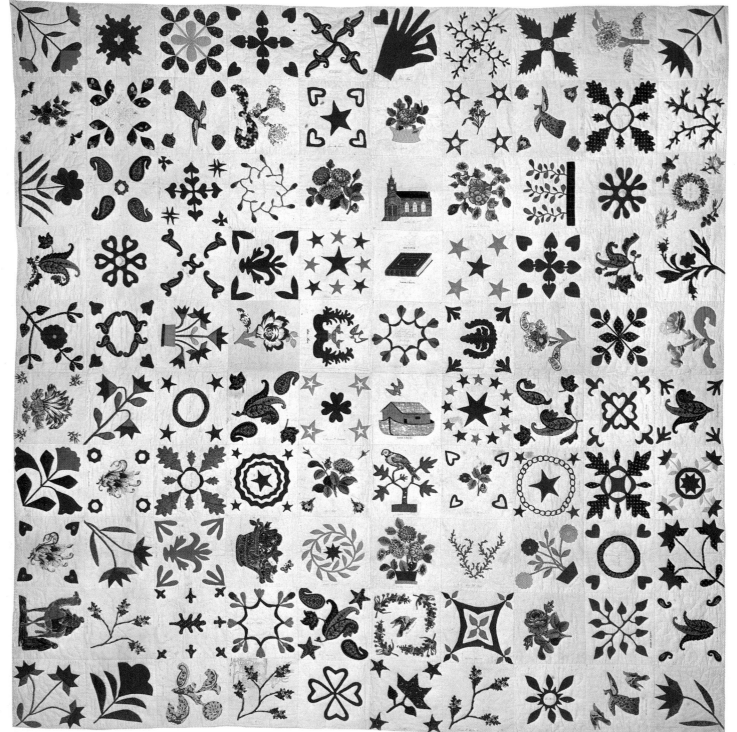

THE APPLIQUÉ QUILT

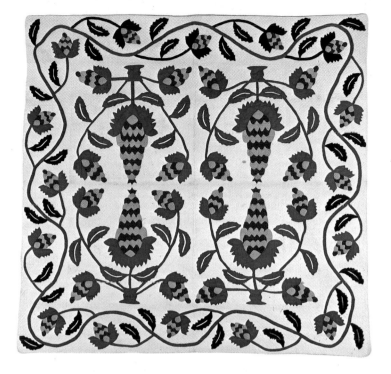

The appliqué quilt was made by carefully cutting designs from a piece of cloth and stitching them onto a plain background. An alternate method was to appliqué a single design onto a block which, in turn, was stitched to several other blocks to form a quilt top.

A very popular type of appliqué quilt was the Album quilt. Many of the most impressive and beautiful Album quilts appear to have been created in or near Baltimore during the first half of the nineteenth century (see figures 108 and 109). Because many appliqué quilts from Maryland have incredibly complex motifs that are nearly identical, it is believed that the motifs were drawn by professionals and purchased by quilters for home use.

Most traditional appliqué patterns continue to be popular with quilters today. The sociable quilting bee has also been revived, and in both rural and urban areas women gather together to stitch heirlooms for future generations. Also, because interest in contemporary quilts is so strong, many needleworkers have formed cooperatives that produce quilts to be sold in retail outlets. Over eighty-five black women are members of the Martin Luther King Freedom Quilting Bee in Alabama, and another successful network of cooperatives throughout the South is Mountain Artisans.

107 (below). Quilting templates, Pennsylvania. When patterns were unperforated, they were used to cut out appliqués; when they contained tiny holes like these, they could also be used to transfer quilting designs to the quilt top. (Phyllis Haders)

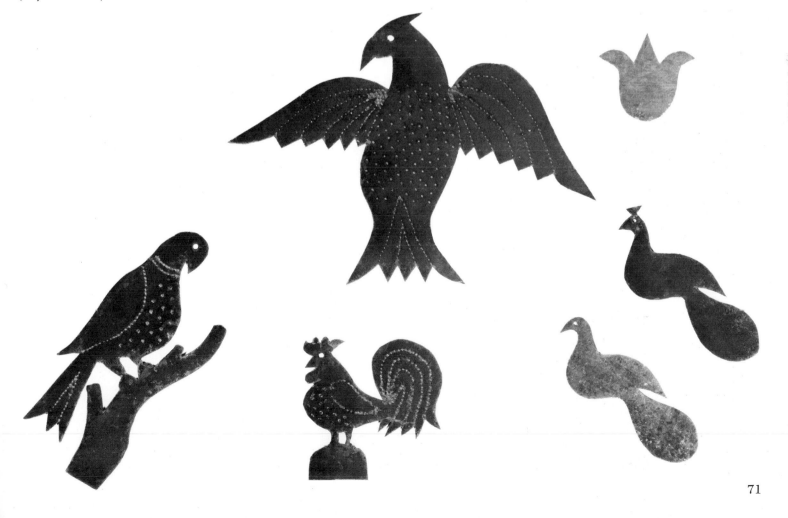

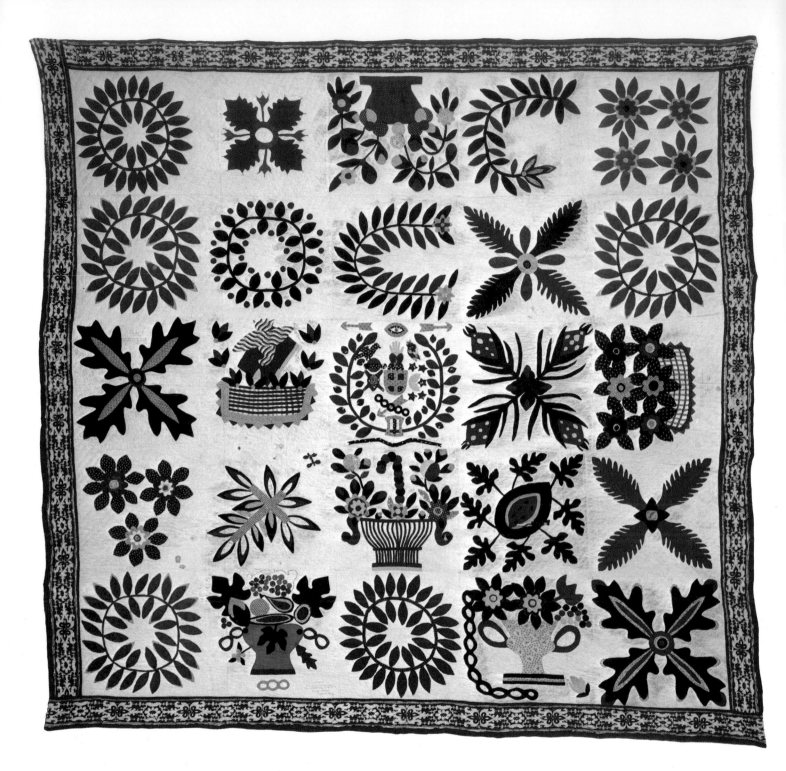

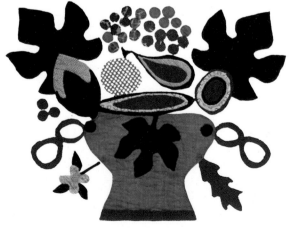

108 (above), 108a (left). Appliqué quilt, Friendship Album, probably Baltimore, dated 1851 and inscribed "For Dr. Lees." 90" x 88¾". This quilt is made from blocks that have been appliquéd with designs. In some quilts these blocks are divided by narrow bands of a single-colored fabric that are called sets. The designs in this beautiful example tend to form an overall pattern because the set device was not used. Note the hand and heart and all-seeing eye in the central block and the handsome print that forms the border. (Private collection)

109 (below), 109a (left). Appliqué quilt, Friendship Album, probably Baltimore, 1850–1860. As can readily be seen from these splendid examples, the Baltimore-type quilt reveled in brilliant color and complex design. This quilt also has a heart-and-hand motif in the center. In the chapter "Decorative Art Needle-Work" of *Our Homes and Their Adornments* Charles E. Bentley says: ". . . Materials of inferior quality should never be chosen. Labor expended on them never pays. The fabrics, of whatever material, should be firm, well woven, and devoid of irregularities. Inexpensive stuffs, when suitably treated and used for appropriate purposes, are just as desirable as more costly ones."[16] (Betty Sterling)

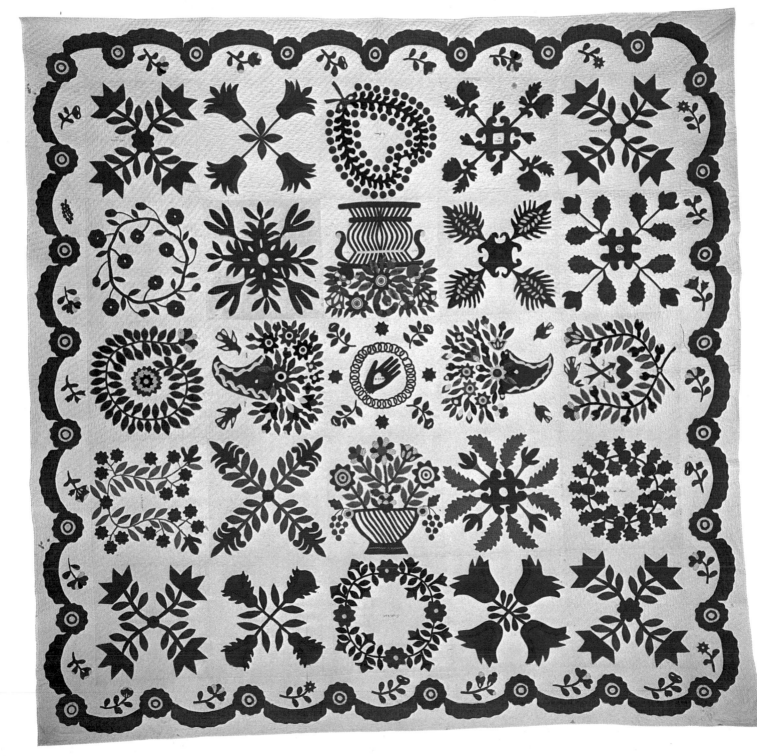

110 (below). Appliqué quilt, Cactus Rose, Pennsylvania, c. 1855. 86″ x 86″. All three quilts on these two pages are notable for their fine quilting. The boldly designed example below with the pieced Lemoyne Star in the center has been finely quilted in parallel diagonal lines. The magnificent Pennsylvania quilt at the top of page 75 has exquisite feather quilting that greatly enhances the overall design of the piece. The third quilt, figure 112, is most unusual, for all of the quilting has been done by machine. Narrowly spaced parallel lines divide the white background into squares and triangles, and even finer machine quilting follows the contours of the appliquéd designs. The reader should apply a magnifying glass to figures 111 and 112 to appreciate fully the quality of the work in them. (America Hurrah Antiques)

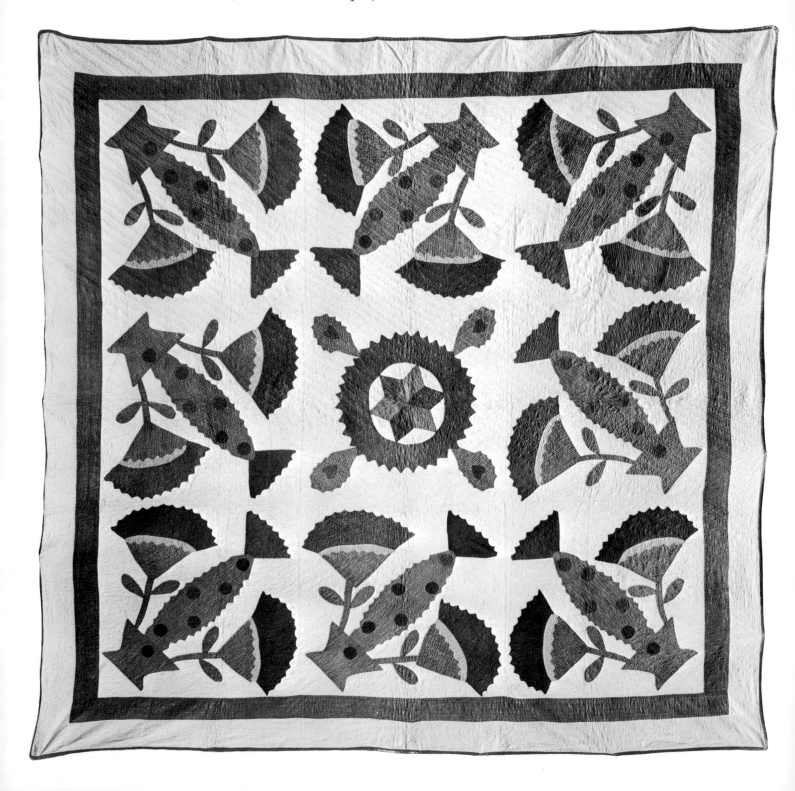

111 (left), 111a (center). Appliqué quilt, Coxcomb, Pennsylvania, 1860–1870. 102″ x 102″. Color, design, needlework—and thirty-four birds—all make this an exceptionally fine Pennsylvania quilt. (Mr. and Mrs. John Borg)

112 (right). Appliqué quilt, Coxcomb and Rose Cross, Portsmouth, New Hampshire, 1900–1910. 77⅛″ x 75¾″. Even though it has been done by machine, the quilting in this piece is so fine that it has the feel of handwork. (Private collection)

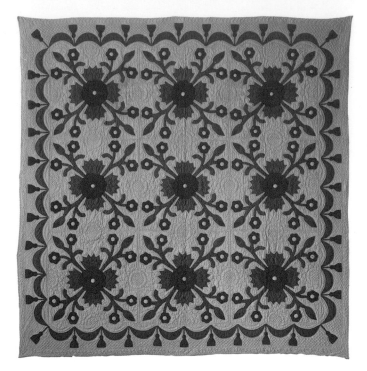

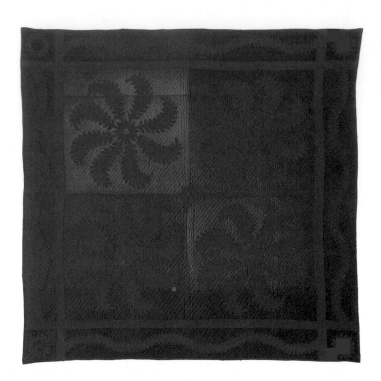

113 (above). Appliqué quilt, Thistle, Pennsylvania, c. 1865. 82" x 80". The flowers are given a three-dimensional effect by the use of padding. (Phyllis Haders)

114 (below). Appliqué quilt, Rose, Pennsylvania, 1870–1880. 90" x 90". (America Hurrah Antiques)

115 (above, right). Appliqué quilt, Princess Feather, c. 1890. The bold colors of this piece match the boldness of the swirling feathers and the undulating border. The eight-pointed star in the center gives the feeling of firmly anchoring all the motion. (George E. Schoellkopf Gallery)

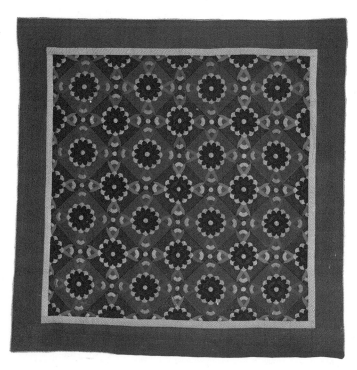

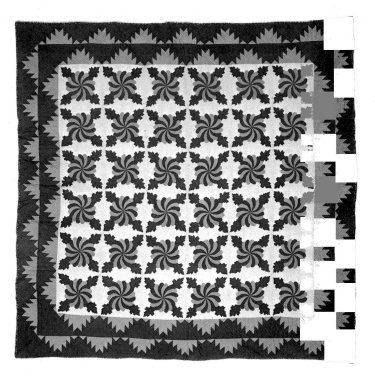

116 (above). Appliqué quilt, Pinwheel and Oak Leaf with Delectable Mountains border, New England, c. 1880. 88" x 88¾". The entire piece is delectable, not just the mountains! (Cora Ginsburg)

117 (below), 117a (right). Appliqué and pieced quilt, Pennsylvania, c. 1865. 78¼" x 78¼". This complex quilt combines several familiar designs that have been assembled in a unique way. The central panel is a one-piece appliqué that is reminiscent of several Hawaiian designs. The pieced borders are in the Wild Goose Chase and Sawtooth patterns. An outer border has appliquéd scallops that are interrupted at the four corners by calico birds. (America Hurrah Antiques)

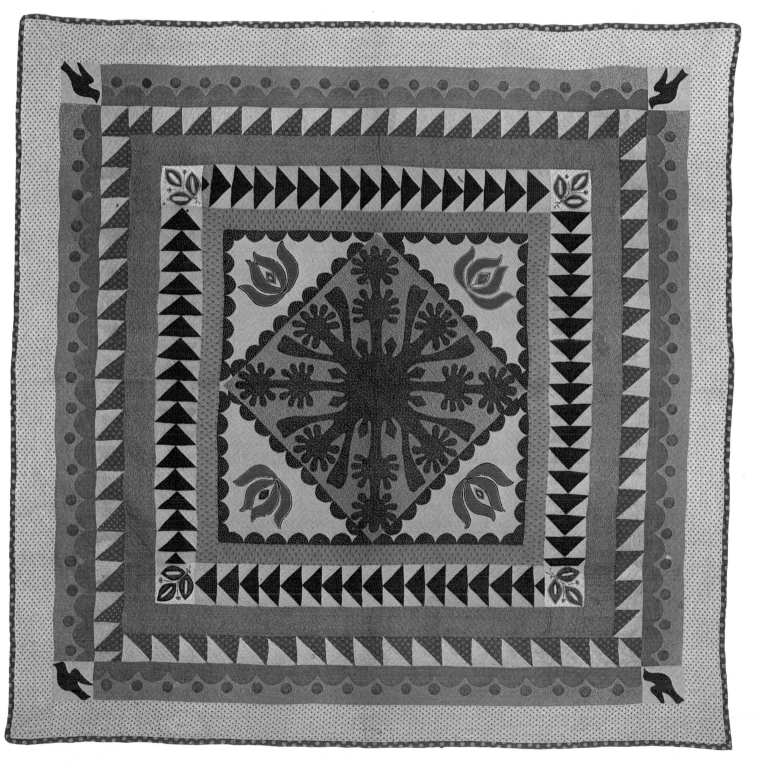

118 (below). Appliqué quilt, Bay Leaf variation, New Jersey, 1850–1860. The fascinating border on this distinctive quilt is in a zigzag design with appliquéd birds in flight on the outer edge and birds at rest on the inner edge. The calicoes used for the birds are particularly interesting. (The Pink House)

119, 119a (opposite). Appliqué quilt, Flowerpots with Birds and a Coxcomb Vine border, 1840–1850. 78″ x 93″. In addition to being a stunning quilt this piece has the added interest of having plants that bear three types of blooms at the same time—a rose, a tulip, and a lily. The jaunty bird is rather similar to the designs used by village blacksmiths when making weathervanes. (Cora Ginsburg)

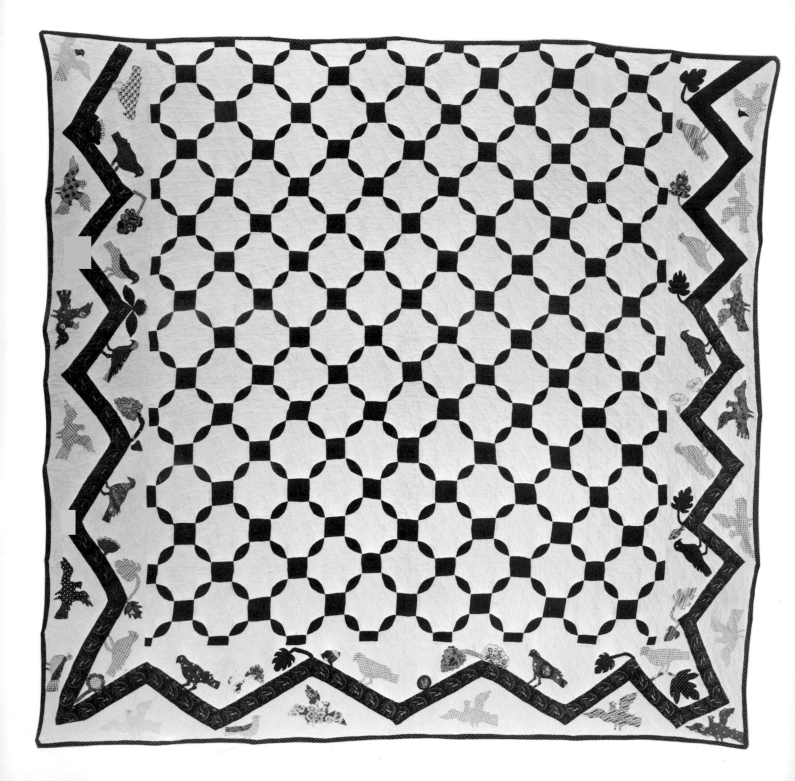

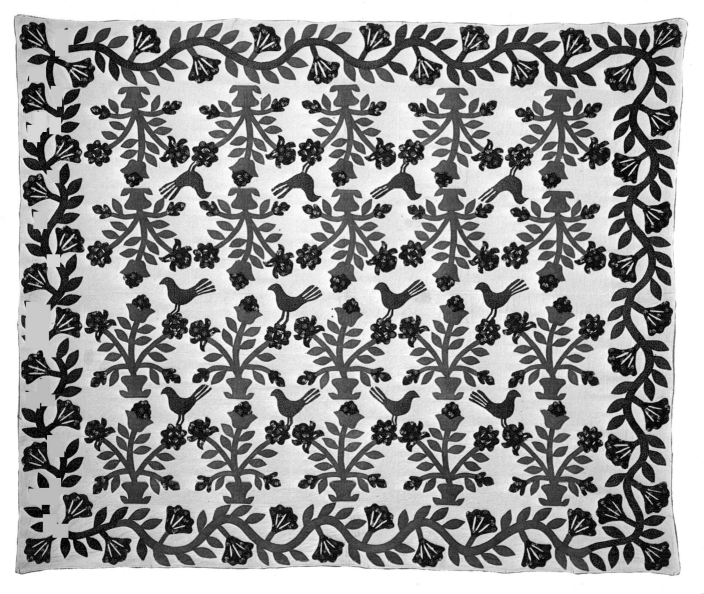

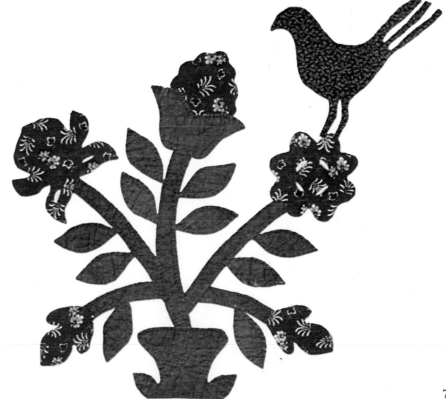

79

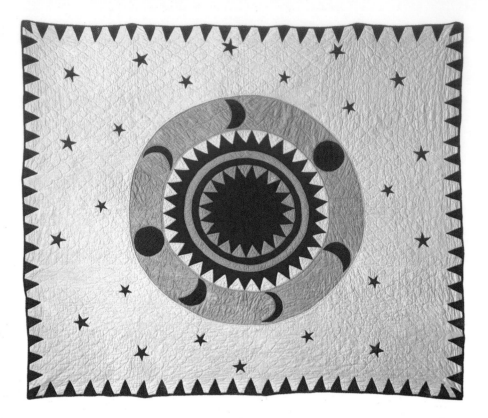

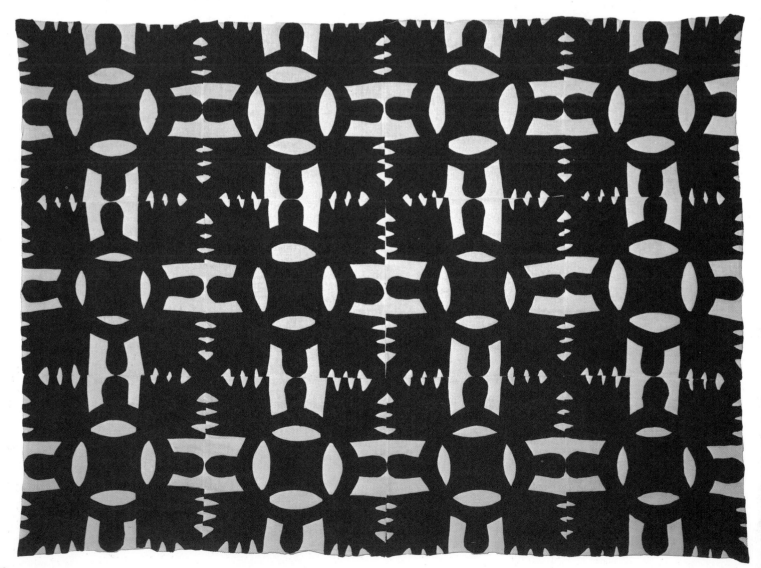

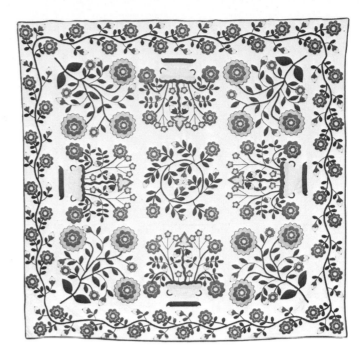

120 (opposite, above). Appliqué and pieced quilt, Sun, Moon, and Stars, New York, dated 1861. Julia Leggett signed this piece, and she could be proud of its beautiful design. (Joanna S. Rose; photograph courtesy America Hurrah Antiques)

121 (opposite, below). Appliqué quilt top, c. 1900. 54″ x 71″. The bold color and design of this quilt top give it an almost contemporary feeling. (Leo and Dorothy Rabkin)

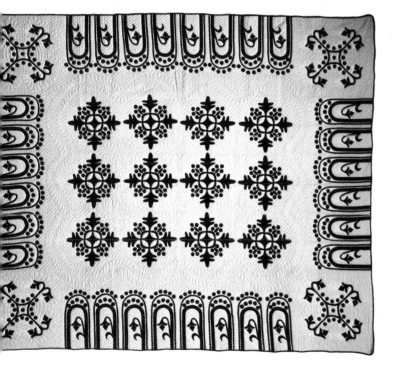

123 (above). Appliqué quilt, Primrose, made by Mrs. Agnes St. Peter, Cheboygan, Michigan, c. 1925. 90″ x 90″. (Mr. and Mrs. James O. Keene)

122 (left), 122a (below). Appliqué quilt, Oak Leaf and Currants with Lily-of-the-Valley border, Trenton, New Jersey, area, c. 1910. 84¾″ x 100½″. The extraordinary border motif gives an Art Nouveau feeling to this piece. The quilting is also particularly handsome. (Private collection)

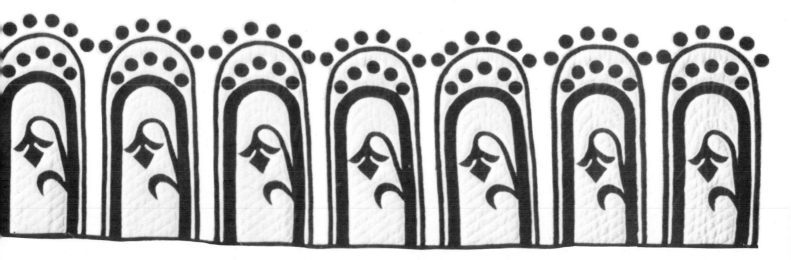

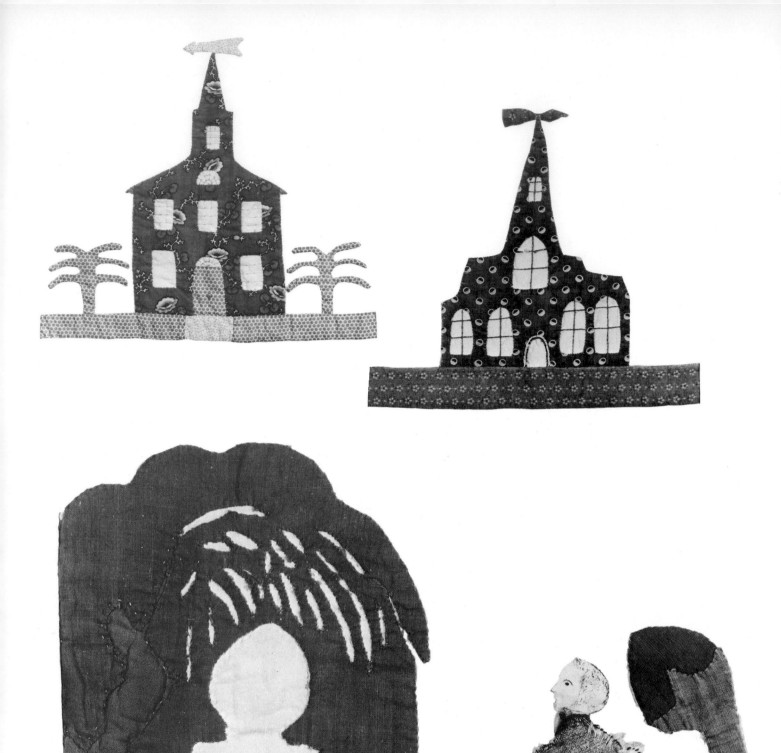

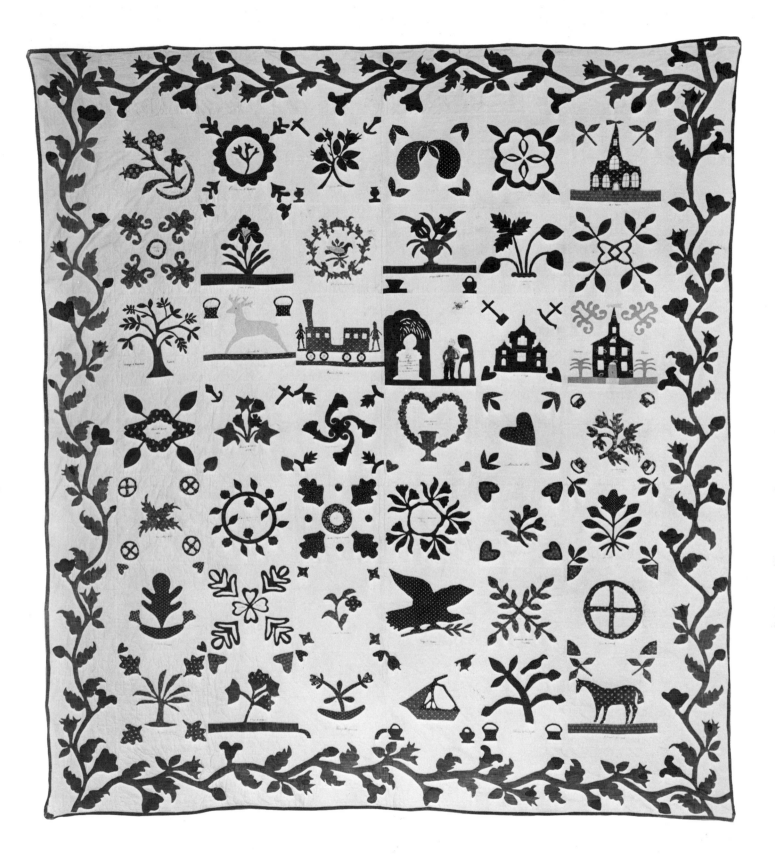

124 (above), 124a, 124b, 124c (opposite). Appliqué quilt, Album, inscribed "P. Thompson Gurney" and dated 1854. 85″ x 73″. This superior example of American folk art includes several appliqués rarely found in quilts: the church, the school, the mourner at the grave, and the train. The grave scene reminds us of the immense popularity of this subject in paintings and needlework in the nineteenth century. In the same year that this quilt was dated Thoreau had this to say about the importance of the train in nineteenth-century life:

". . . when I hear the iron horse make the hills echo with his snort like thunder, shaking the earth with his feet, and breathing fire and smoke from his nostrils, it seems as if the earth had got a race now worthy to inhabit it. . . . The startings and arrivals of the cars are now the epochs in the village day. They go and come with such regularity and precision, and their whistle can be heard so far, that the farmers set their clocks by them, and thus one well-conducted institution regulates a whole country."[17] (Marguerite Riordan)

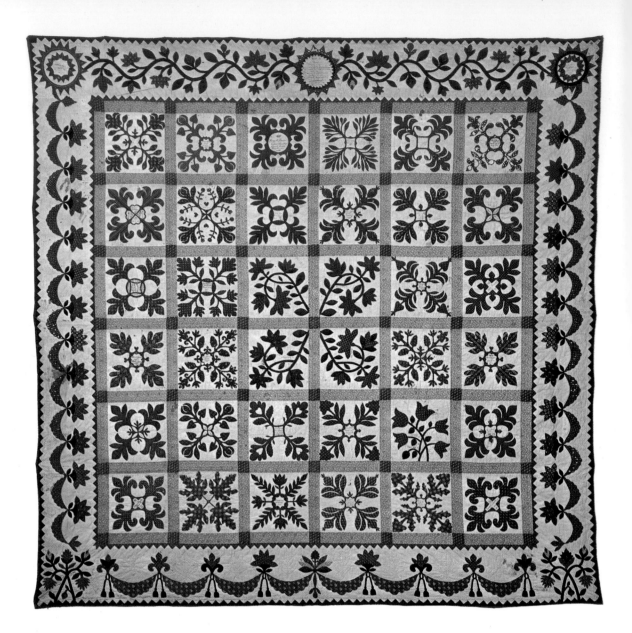

125 (above), 125a (left). Appliqué quilt, Album, made by Sarah Holcomb, Lancaster County, Pennsylvania, dated March 9, 1847. 95" x 95". Sarah Holcomb made this exquisite piece "In rememberence of her Friends and Relations." In the circular panel at the center of the top border, which is enlarged at left, there is this further inscription: "It is religion that must give sweetest / Pleasure while we live / It is religion that must supply / Solid comfort, when we die / For after death its joys shall be / Lasting as eternity / When this you see / Remember me." Note the effective, small touches of yellow used in the border designs. (Private collection)

126 (opposite, above). Appliqué quilt, New York, c. 1875. 81½" x 64¾". (Thos. K. Woodard: American Antiques & Quilts)

127 (opposite, below). Appliqué quilt, Pennsylvania, c. 1850. 89" x 68". This quilt and that in figure 126 were probably intended as bride's coverlets, since the heart motif is abundantly used in both. A pineapple motif is also incorporated into the six central blocks of this quilt. (America Hurrah Antiques)

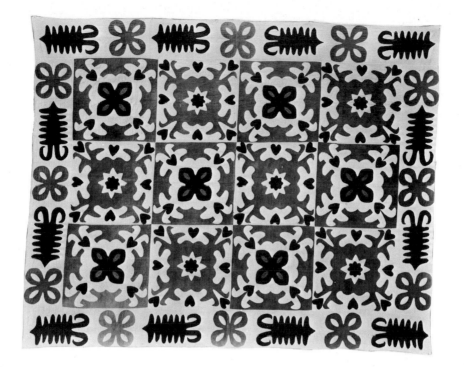

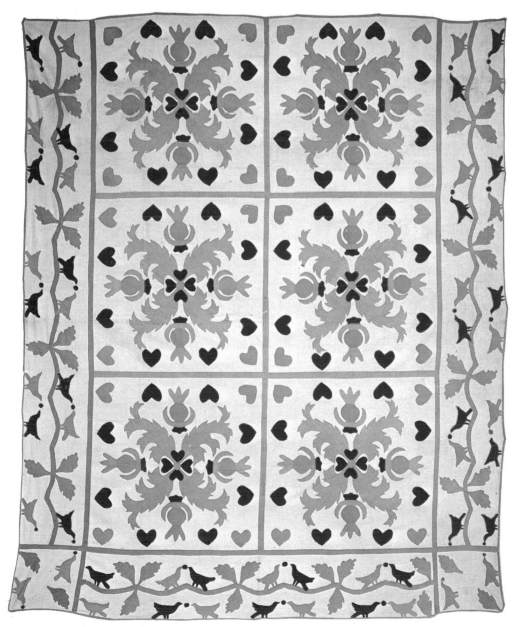

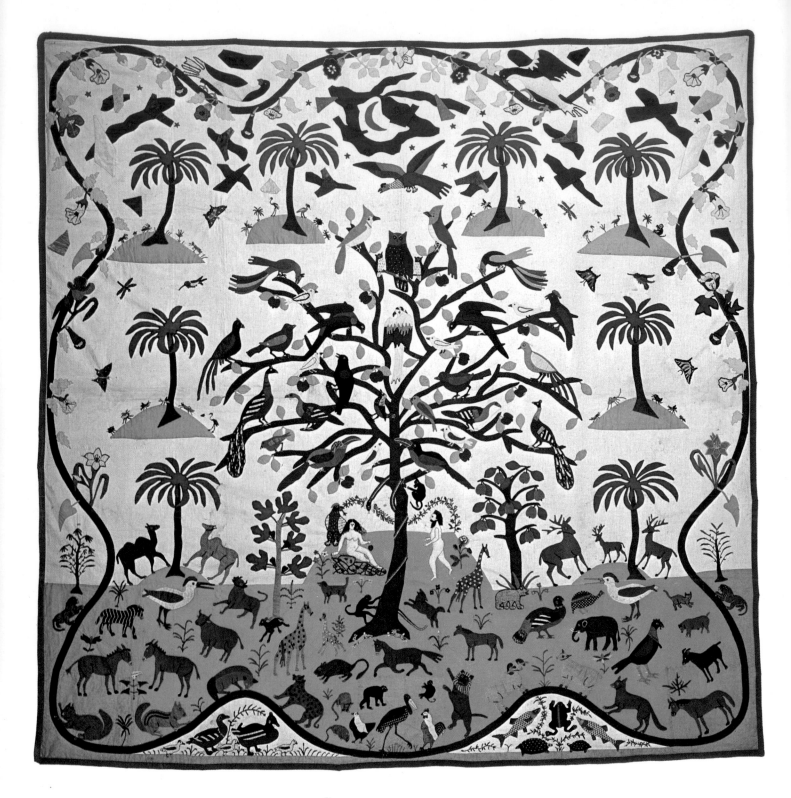

128 (above). Appliqué quilt, Garden of Eden, made by Abby F. Bell Ross, Irvington, New Jersey, dated 1874. 87″ x 87″. To say the least, this is an incredible production in terms of design, color, and sheer multiplicity of images. The maker obviously was an ambitious needlewoman, and it is safe to say that her vision of Adam and Eve and the Tree of Life in Paradise is uniquely successful. (Mr. and Mrs. Ben Mildwoff; photograph courtesy John Gordon)

129 (below). Appliqué and pieced quilt, variation of Mexican Rose, Ohio, 1850–1860.
93″ x 76″. Color, movement, and design—all these elements are marvelously combined in this
great quilt. (The Pink House)

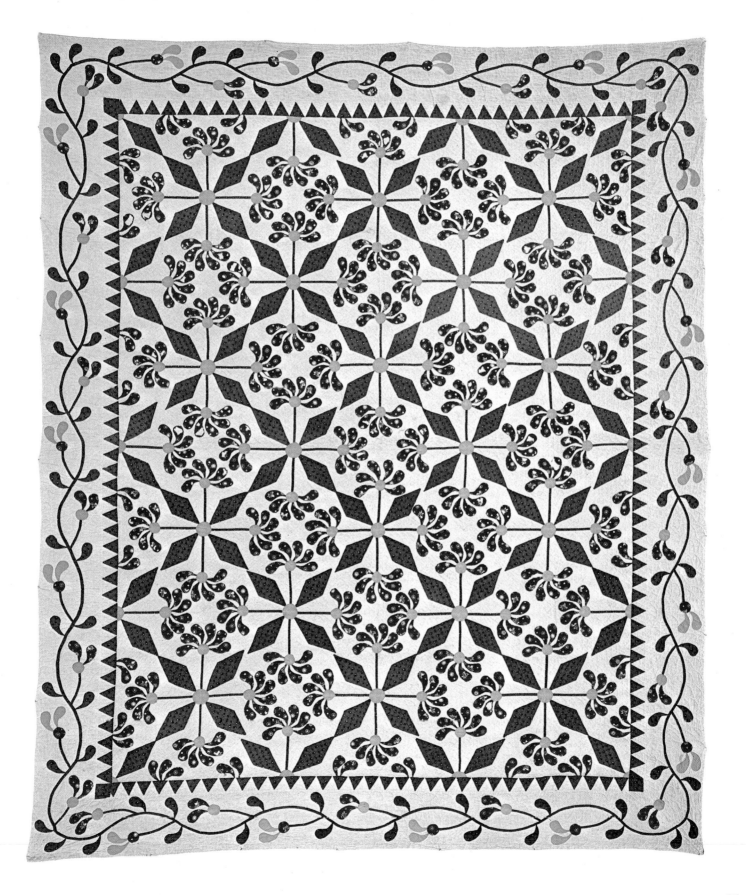

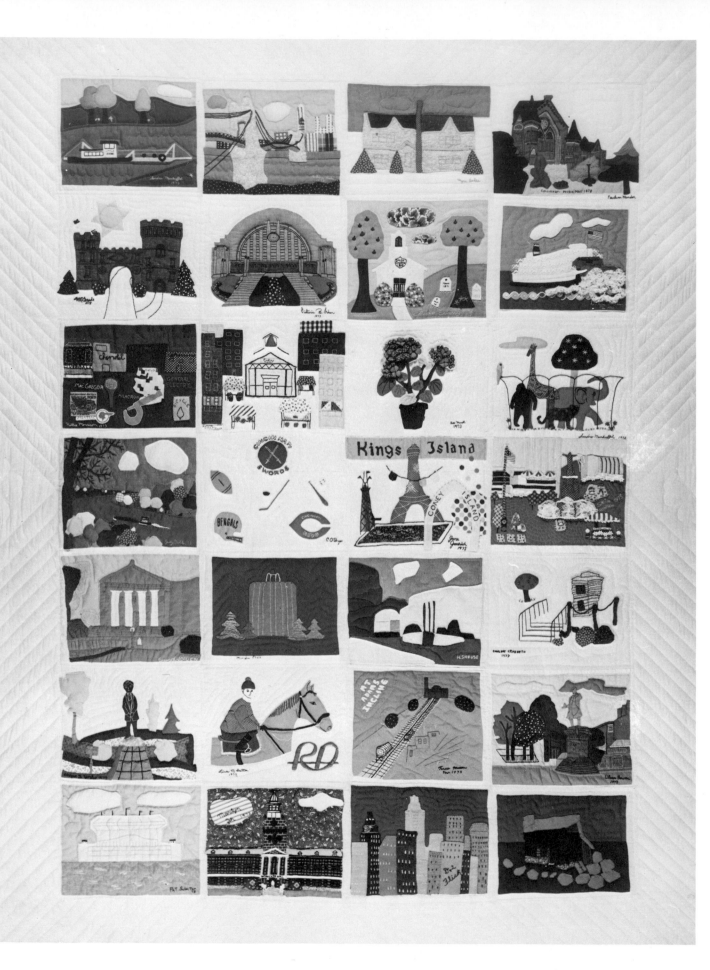

130 (opposite). Appliqué quilt made by the Anderson High School Adult Education Class, Cincinnati, Ohio, 1974. 115″ x 90″. In anticipation of the national Bicentennial many quilting groups have commemorated some of the most distinctive features of their cities through pictorial appliqués. (City of Cincinnati; photograph courtesy Cincinnati Art Museum)

131 (right). Quilt made in 1974 by Karee Skarsten from photographs silk-screened on fabric, machine quilted. Buffalo, New York. 81″ x 75½″. The artist has with great imagination used the profile of an oil refinery to form her borders; the repeated motif of the blocks in the central section is the stair that curves up the side of a storage tank. This is a fine example of the way in which the industrial landscape can be transmuted into an object of real beauty. (Karee Skarsten)

132 (below). Members of the Urban Quilt Workshop completing the New York City Bicentennial Community Quilt containing forty pictorial blocks. One of the workers on the quilt exclaimed: "I really wish we could put it in a time capsule, or better yet, let's hang it from the Brooklyn Bridge!" (New York City Bicentennial Commission)

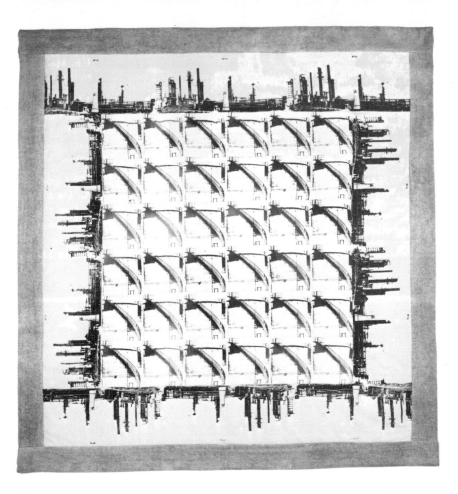

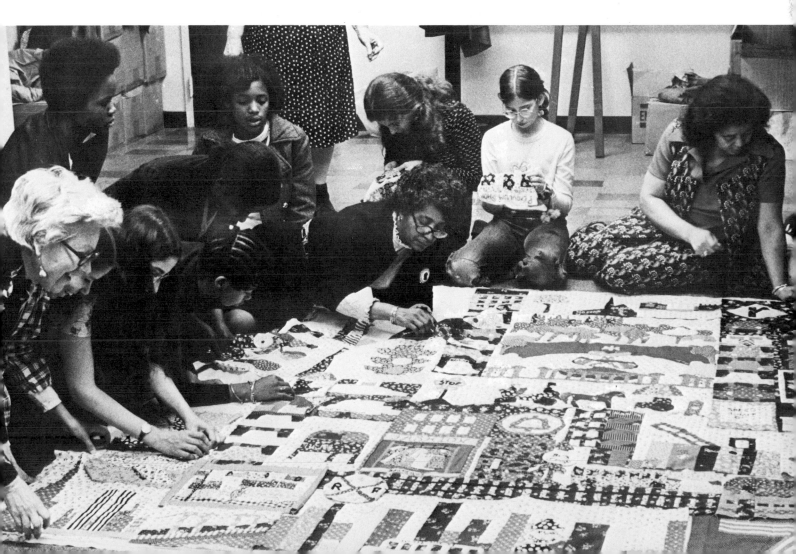

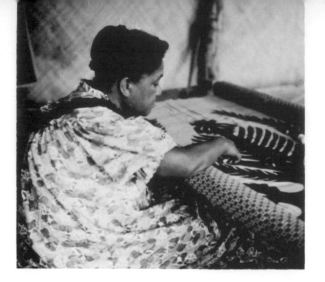

133 (left). A Hawaiian woman demonstrates the art of quilting at Ulu Mau village. Hawaiian quilts continue to be made in the traditional patterns. (Mauna Kea Beach Hotel, Hawaii)

134 (below). Appliqué quilt in the design called *Ke Kahi o Kaiulani* (The Comb of Kaiulani), Hawaii, before 1918. 88½″ x 84″. The quilting has been done in horizontal and vertical parallel lines. The background is white cotton; the appliqué was cut from wine-red cotton. (Honolulu Academy of Arts; Gift of Mrs. Richard A. Cooke)

135 (opposite, above). Appliqué quilt in the design called *Ka Ua Kani Lehua* (The Rain that Rustles Lehua Blossoms), Hawaii, before 1900. 83″ x 78″. This quilt has yellow cotton appliqués on a red cotton background, and the quilting is in concentric ridges that conform to the contours of the design. (Honolulu Academy of Arts; Gift of Damon Giffard)

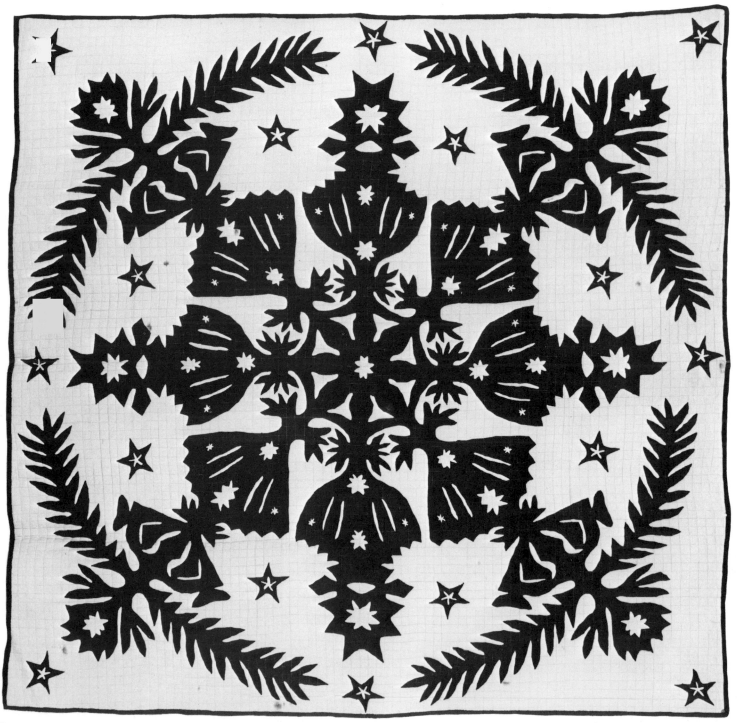

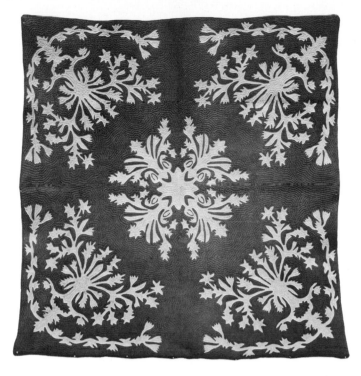

HAWAIIAN QUILTS

Quilting was first introduced to Hawaii on April 3, 1820, by missionaries from New England. Armed with the Bible, religious fervor, and a sense of propriety, zealous gospel spreaders persuaded the natives that they should be ashamed of their nudity. Since Hawaiians were unaccustomed to being fully clothed, the *muu muu*, a loose-fitting garment probably adapted from a simple New England nightgown, was more acceptable than the constricting clothing worn by the missionaries. These *muu muus* were frequently quilted.

Most Hawaiian quilts were fashioned from bolts of a single-color fabric introduced by the New England visitors. Large appliqués of contrasting colors, usually in a single design, sometimes repeated, provided a decorative overlay on neutral backgrounds. The free-form appliqués so popular in Hawaii were usually cut with the aid of a paper pattern that had been snipped from a folded piece of paper. The quilting generally follows the outlines of the appliqué design. The designs are most often inspired by the natural beauty of Hawaii.

During the nineteenth century any Hawaiian home of social pretensions included a quilting frame in the parlor furnishings. Hawaiian women used low frames for they preferred to sit on the ground while they worked. In time, the quilting bee became a prestigious social function. Hawaiian bees were different from those in the States because the woman sponsoring the event never contributed to her own quilt, since her sole function was to prepare the banquetlike meal enjoyed at the end of the day.

Today, Hawaiian ladies from numerous church and civic societies continue to fashion quilts as part of their fund-raising efforts.

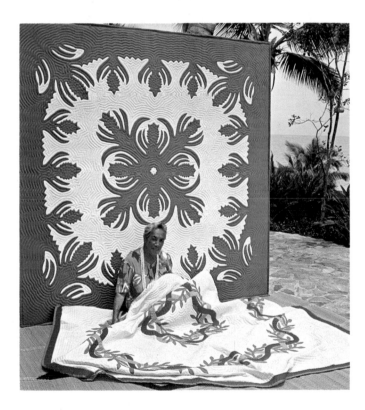

136 (above). Hawaiian woman with two contemporary quilts. Lawrence S. Rockefeller commissioned quiltmakers of Honolulu Kawaiahoa Mission Church to create thirty quilts, each approximately eight feet square. The quilt designs derive from Hawaii's natural environment—its flowers, fruits, leaves, famous landmarks, and legends. (Photograph courtesy Mauna Kea Beach Hotel, Hawaii)

137 (right). Appliqué quilt in the traditional Hawaiian pattern called Rain of Honolulu, made by Marie K. Robertom, California, 1974. 76" x 76". (Greenfield Village and Henry Ford Museum)

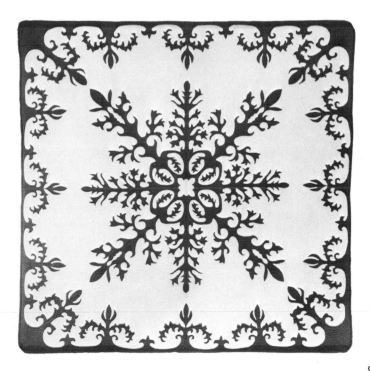

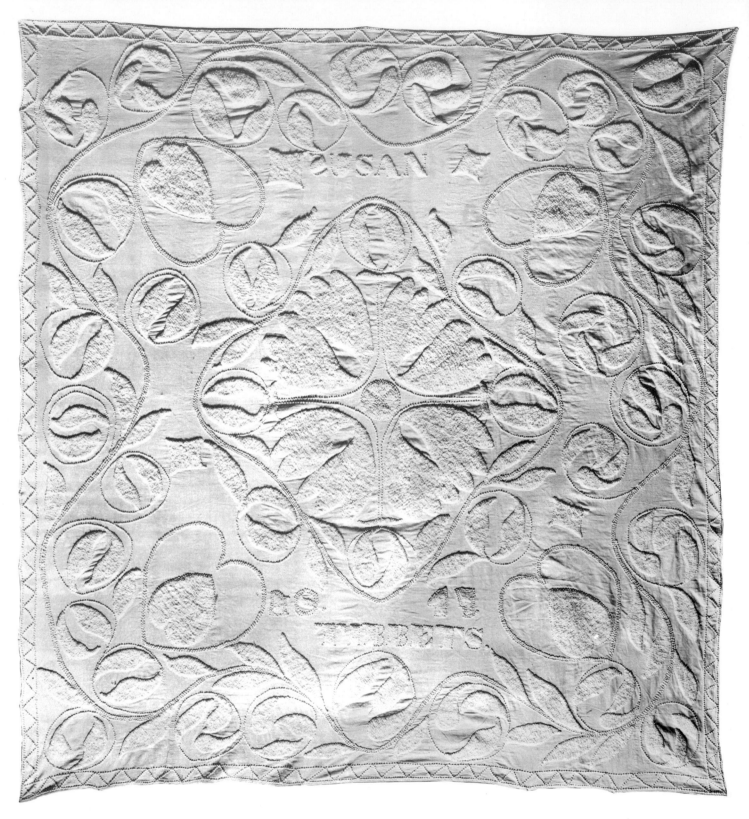

138 (above). Embroidered candlewick spread made by Susan Tibbets, probably New England, dated 1847. This beautiful piece with its rhythmic serpentine lines of French knots was possibly intended to be a marriage spread, since the design includes four large open hearts made of French hearts, each of which encloses a smaller heart made of sheared roving. (Private collection; photograph courtesy George E. Schoellkopf Gallery)

139 (opposite). Embroidered candlewick spread with ribbed-cotton background, New England, 1810–1820. 100″ x 100″. The special beauty and interest of this superb bedcover centers on the elaborate vase-of-flowers motif topped with a small bird. Many of the floral motifs that appear on bed rugs and contemporary crewel-embroidered spreads are found in this piece. Compare the bed rug in figure 2, page 11. (Private collection; photograph courtesy Cora Ginsburg)

THE CANDLEWICK SPREAD

There are two types of candlewick spread—those woven on a loom and those embroidered on a linen or cotton background.

The loom-woven candlewick spread became popular in America about 1820. The weaver picked up predetermined loops of the soft, white, coarse, cotton thread known as candlewicking or roving from the flat weaving with a "reed" that secured the loops while he treadled the warp encircling the wicking. For variation, the weaver might use reeds of varying diameter, allowing him to create contrasting deep-pile and low-pile designs. Presumably, most of the woven candlewicks were made by professionals.

The art of embroidering with roving also became popular and lasted for a much longer period. Figures 138 and 139 show how effectively the needlewoman could create complex, handsome designs with candlewicking. The fuzzy tufts that are used as accents in figure 139 are made from loops of candlewicking that have been sheared.

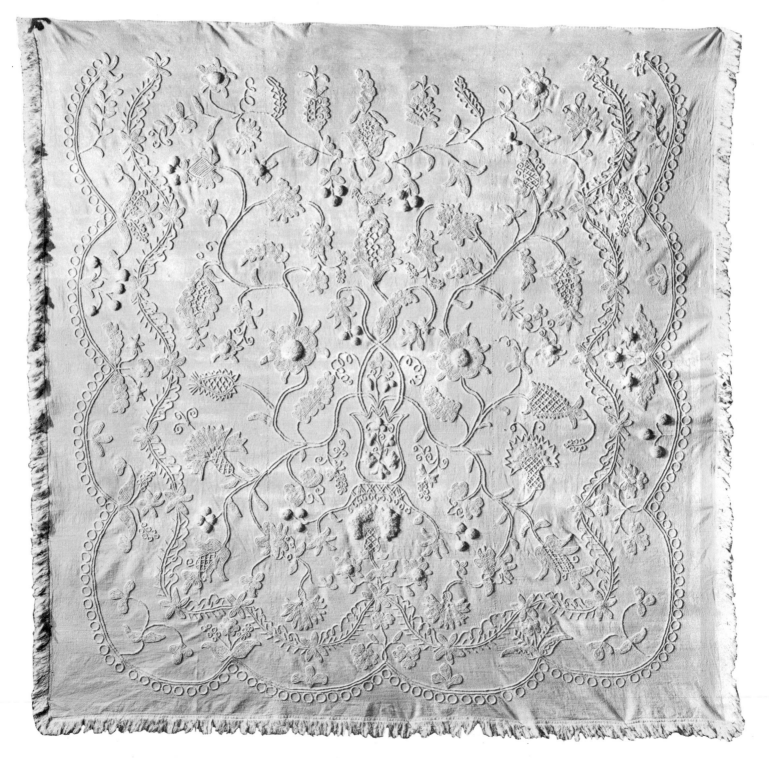

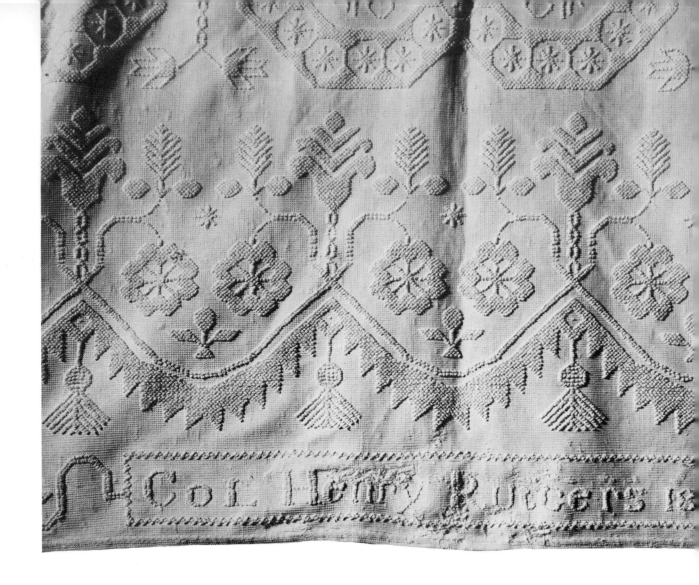

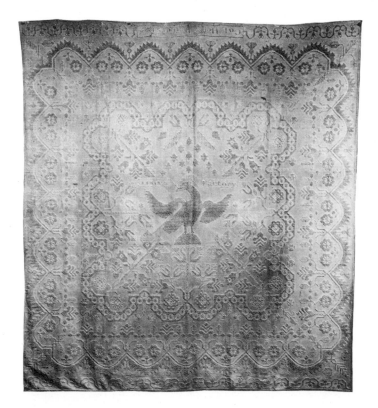

140 (left), 140a (above), 140b (opposite). Woven candlewick spread made at the Rutgers Factory in Paterson, New Jersey, which was owned by Colonel Henry Rutgers. His name and the date 1822 are woven into the spread, as is the additional inscription, "Rutgers Factory," above the eagle. A statistical account of the town of Paterson taken between July 4, 1824, and July 4, 1825, states the following:

Rutgers Factory (cotton) ShawCross & Berry	
Spindles	2300
Cotton Consumed Weekly	24 Cwt
Power Looms	44-42 in operation
Yards of Cloth woven weekly on D⁰ [ditto]	5040
Hands Employed	100
Weekly wages	$275

The Rutgers piece is the most impressive woven candlewick spread that is known. (Mrs. Samuel Schwartz)

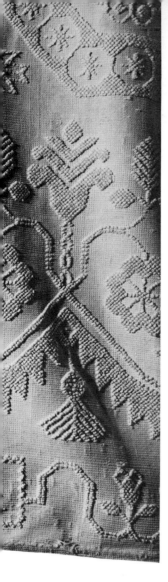

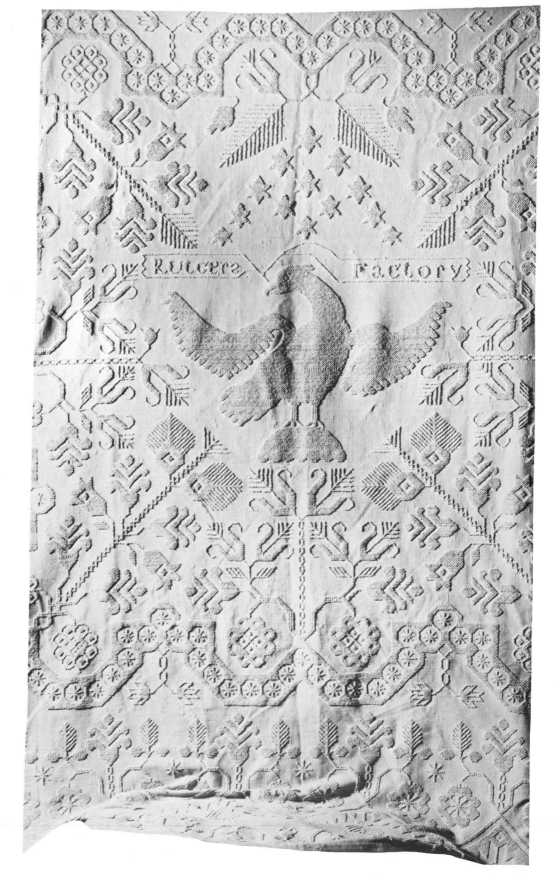

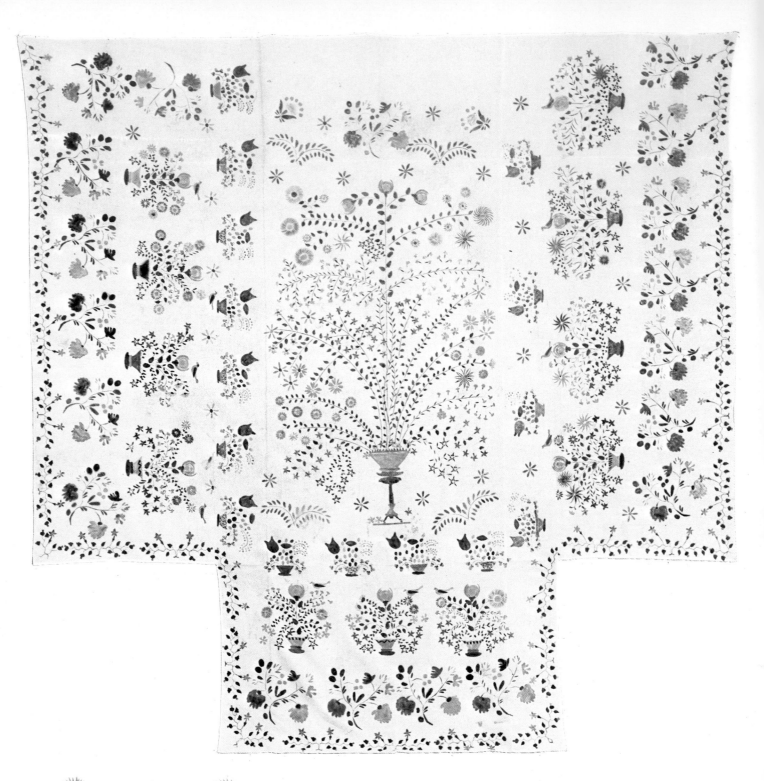

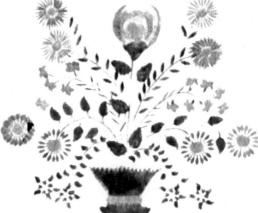

141 (above), 141a (left). Stenciled bedcover made by Emily Morton, Thorndyke, Maine, 1826. 103" x 104". This is an exquisitely designed and painted example. The most usual method of applying the colored design was to mix a stencil mordant, composed of ground pigment and oil, that tended to set the colors permanently. An alternate solution, made from concentrated dye mixed with gum arabic, was preferred by some because it did not run under the edges of the openings in the stencil design and thus create fuzzy edges. (Abby Aldrich Rockefeller Folk Art Collection; Gift of the Estate of Grace Westerfield)

142 (opposite, above). Stencil spread. c. 1835. 89½" x 77½". This example is quilted. (Mr. and Mrs. Foster McCarl, Jr.)

143 (opposite, below). Stencil spread, 1825–1835. 76¼" x 95¼". Here, indeed, is an ebullience of blooms! (Mrs. Samuel Schwartz)

THE STENCIL SPREAD

During the first half of the nineteenth century a taste developed for painted and stenciled furniture, walls, floors, and even spreads.

Nearly all surviving examples of stenciled cotton bedcovers were made without a backing and inner lining and are therefore unquilted. It seems almost certain that stencil spreads were created by women at home and were never produced in large quantities. Designs similar to the flower and fruit still lifes used by young ladies for "theorem" paintings stenciled on velvet and paper were constantly used.

The motifs on the earliest spreads of this type appear to be made up of several small stencils with each contributing part of the overall design. On later examples a single stencil was used; so the motifs tend to be larger and lack variety.

A fine stencil spread only rarely comes to light anymore, and the spread shown in figure 141 is one of the finest examples known to this writer.

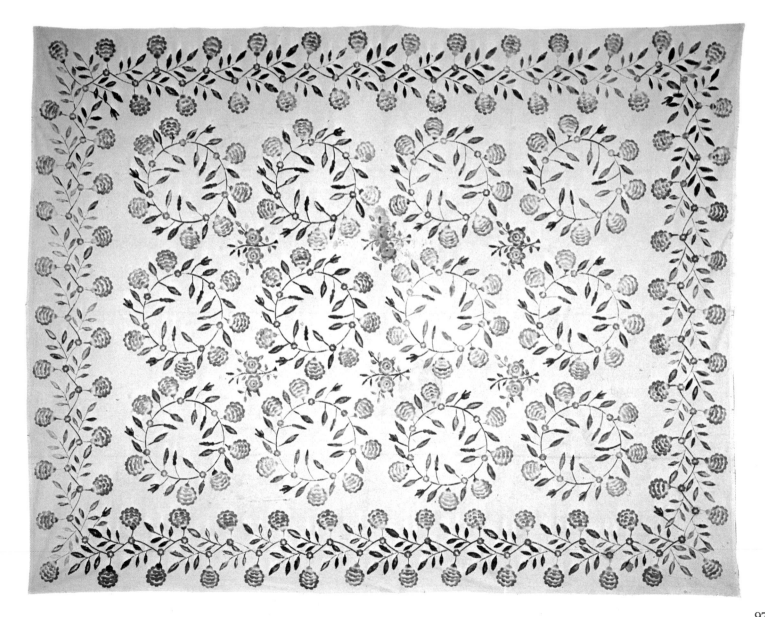

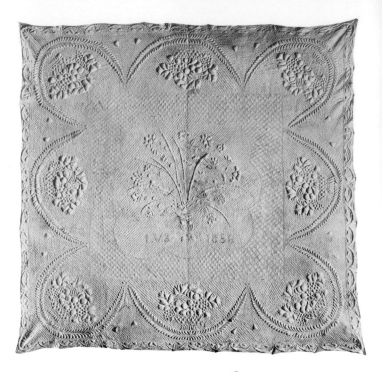

144 (right) and 145 (below). It is probable that these superb examples of stuffed work were made by one person for sisters, for the example in figure 144 is initialed LVB and dated 1856 and that in figure 145 is initialed LCB and dated 1861. Both quilts are also almost exactly alike in design, with the 1861 example being slightly more elaborate and assured than the earlier piece. Both are from New York State. Figure 144 measures 86″ x 88″; figure 145 is 88″ x 90″. (America Hurrah Antiques)

146 (opposite). Crib quilt of white stuffed work, New England, c. 1825. 38½″ x 38½″. The baskets of plump fruit and the grapes of plenty seen in this quilt are ancient motifs found constantly in American needlework. The quilt is finished on three sides by an elaborate border of fringed netting. (America Hurrah Antiques)

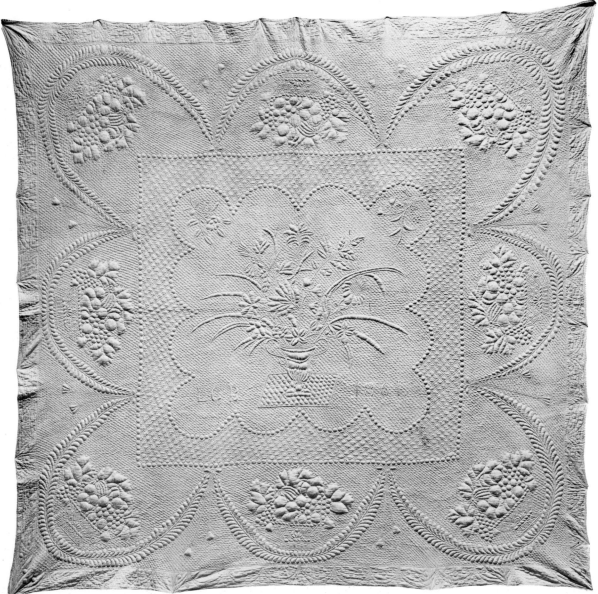

STUFFED WORK

All-white bedcovers fashioned from a single piece of cotton or linen and elaborately quilted and stuffed are usually referred to as stuffed work or trapunto. This type of quilt was probably the most difficult of all to make, as the illustrations will testify. Elaborate needlework masterworks like these were attempted only by the very skilled and ambitious.

Many quilts with appliqué designs of colored fabric were also stuffed. Examples will be found on pages 102–103. As in the all-white quilts, the threads on the coarser backing of the quilt were carefully separated and cotton or batting was pushed through the hole. When the desired fullness had been achieved, the threads were pulled together again. After washing, the strained threads generally shrank together tightly, thus firmly securing the stuffing inside.

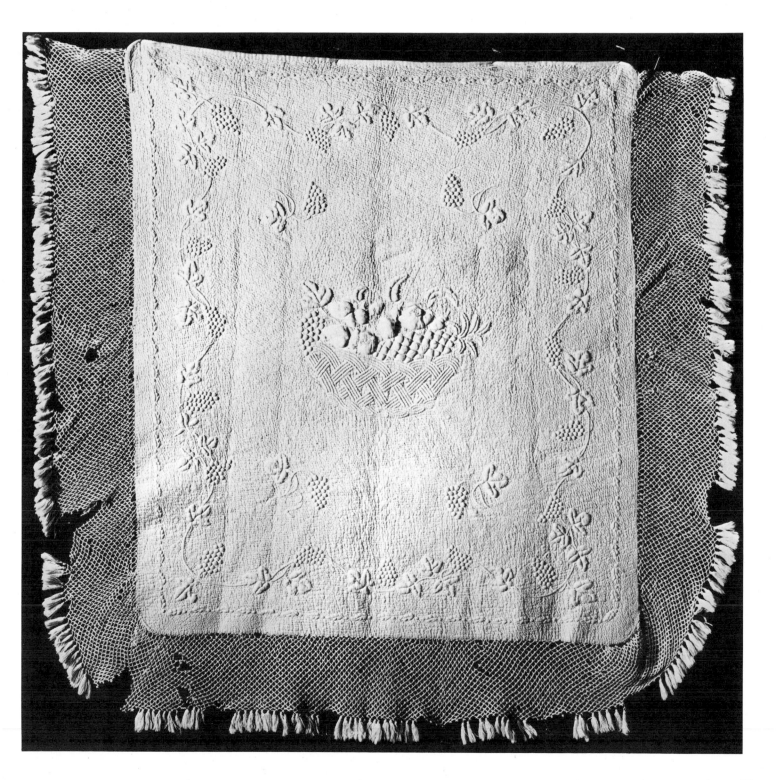

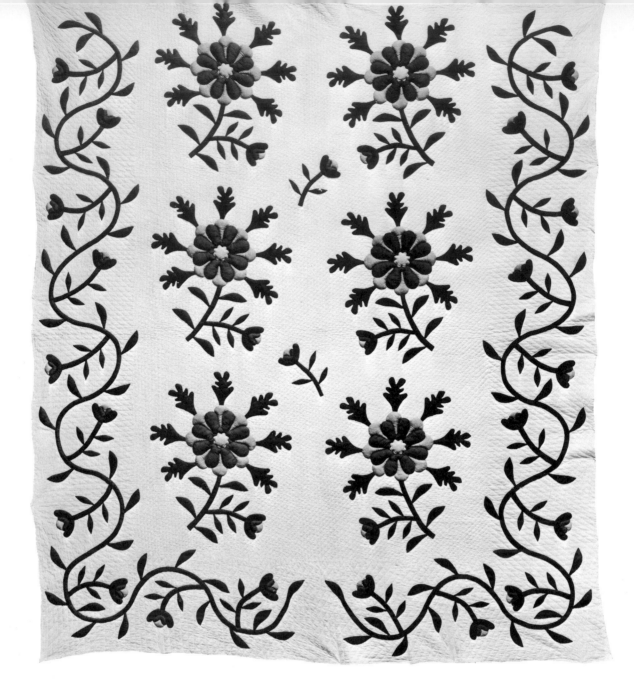

147 (above). Appliqué quilt with red-and-green stuffed work, northern New England, c. 1850. 90″ x 74″. The stuffed work in this piece is raised well above the background giving a very sculptural effect to the design. (Private collection)

148 (right), 148a (opposite). Appliqué quilt with stuffed-work panels and border, 1845–1855. 78″ x 76″. The appliqué design is called California Rose. The fineness of the quilting and stuffing in this masterful example is quite breathtaking, as can be appreciated from studying the detail on the page opposite. (American Hurrah Antiques)

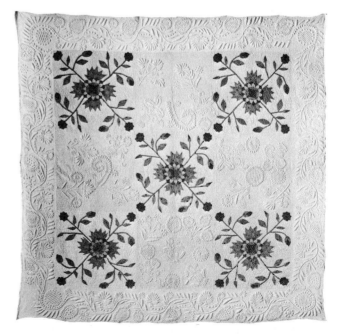

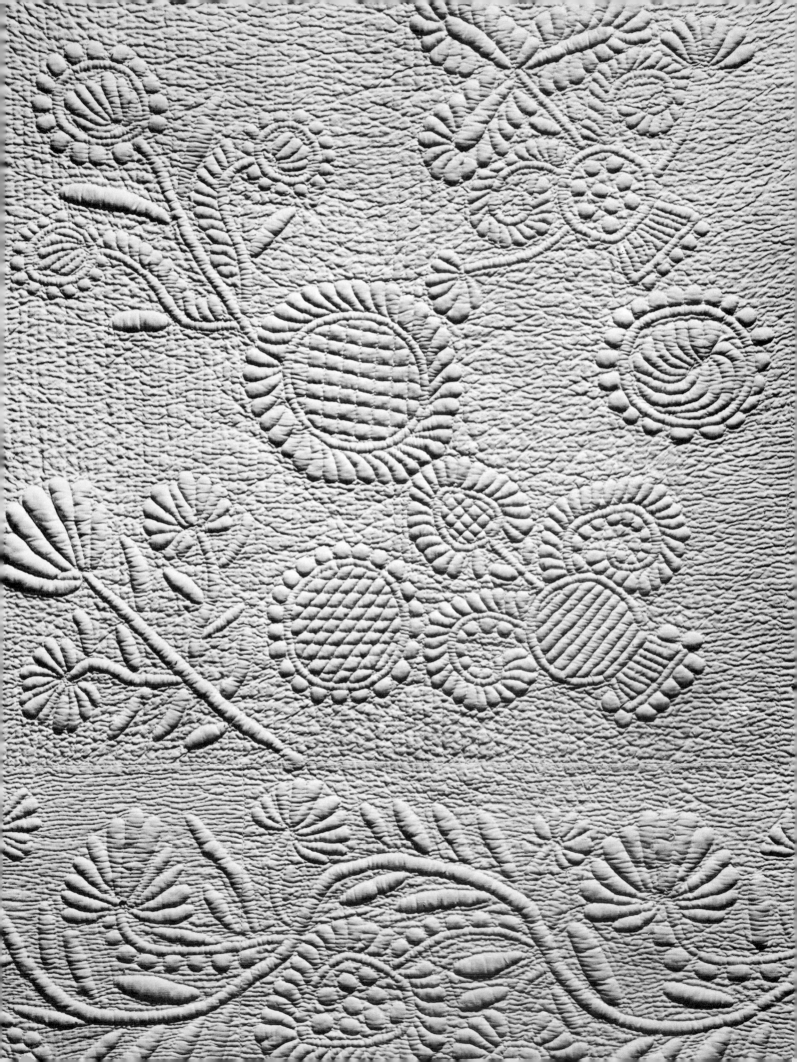

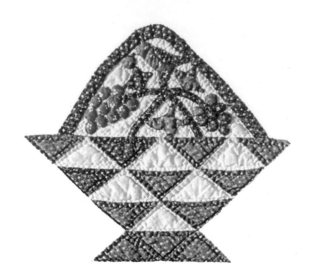

149 (below), 149a (left). Pieced and appliqué quilt, Flower Basket, New England, c. 1870. 90" x 100". In this marvelous piece the elements of the border and the motifs placed under the basket handles are stuffed. The quilting is especially fine, and it includes a pineapple of hospitality in each of the four corners of the wide border. The Flower Basket is one of the most popular designs found in pieced quilts. Another vibrant example of this pattern is seen in figure 56, page 43. (Betty Sterling; photograph courtesy Mr. and Mrs. Leonard Balish)

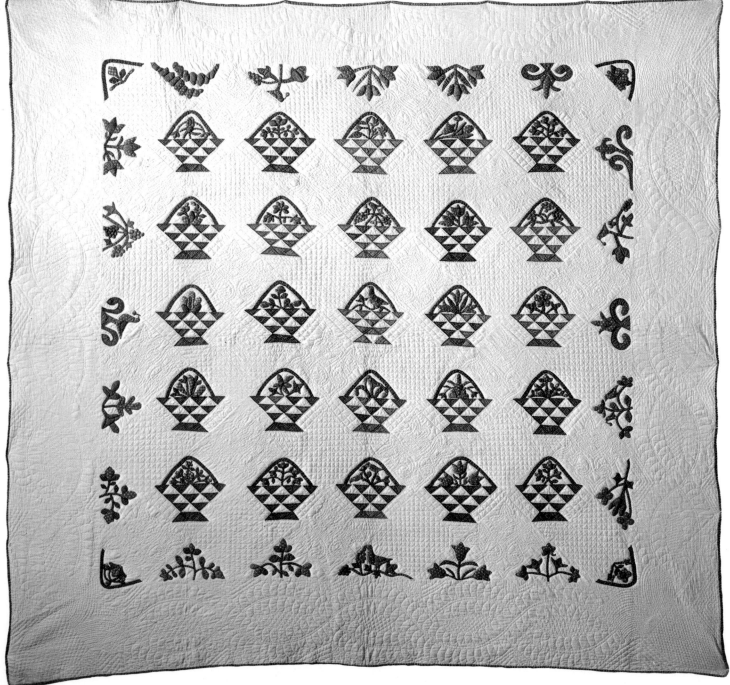

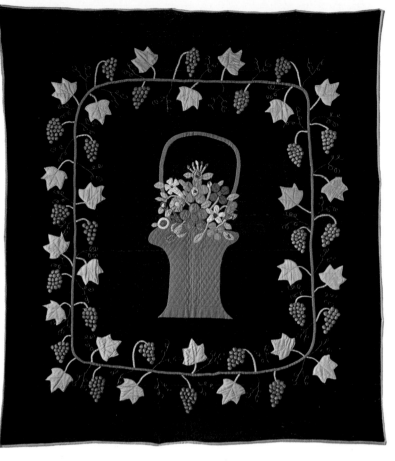

150 (below). Pieced and stuffed quilt, variation of Whig's Defeat, probably New England, 1850–1860. 92" x 91½". Running diamond sets separate the circular motifs and form the border. The fine stuffed work in several floral patterns sets off the pieced work. (Cora Ginsburg)

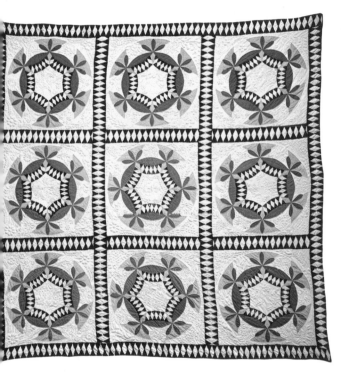

151 (above, right). Appliqué quilt with border of stuffed grapes, Pennsylvania, c. 1920. 76" x 68". (Private collection; photograph courtesy Kelter-Malcé Antiques)

152 (right). Appliqué quilt with stuffed work, Pennsylvania, dated 1862. 79" x 74". Four identical vases of flowers form the central motifs of this very beautiful example of Pennsylvania color and design. Tiny vases with flattened bouquets form the borders. All the cherries are stuffed. (Mr. and Mrs. Edwin Braman)

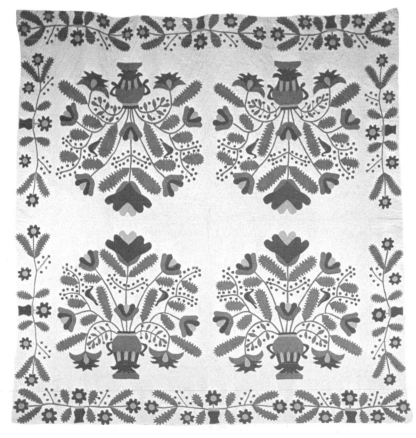

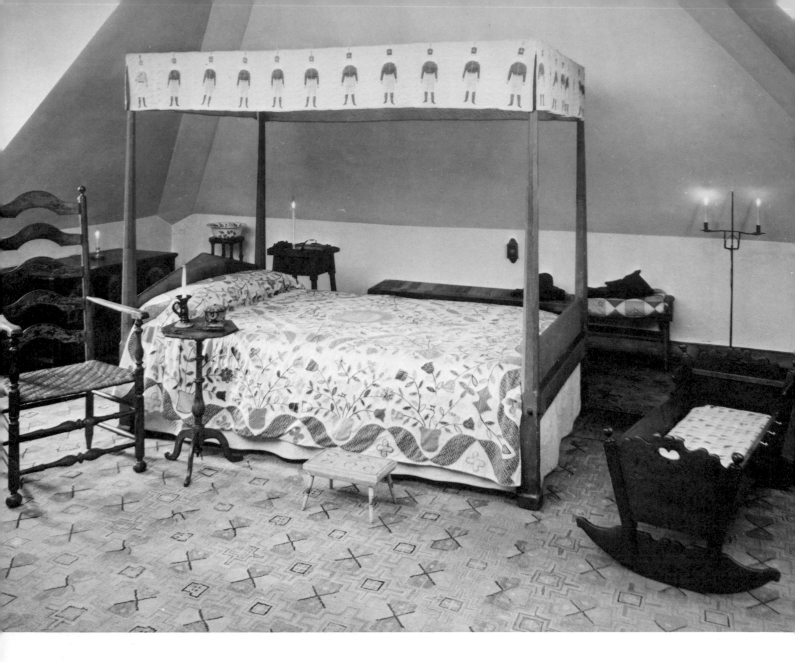

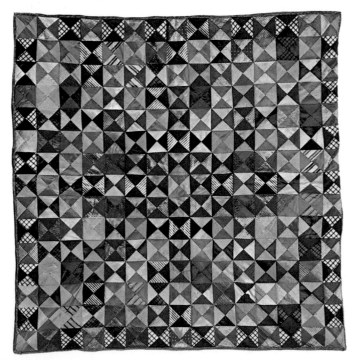

153 (above). Child's bedroom featuring a walnut bed made in Pennsylvania between 1770 and 1785. The valance with appliquéd soldiers is dated 1853 and was once part of a bedspread. The Pennsylvania cradle at the foot of the bed has handsome ends and rockers. (The Henry Francis du Pont Winterthur Museum)

154 (left). Pieced crib quilt, Broken Dishes, c. 1850. 32″ x 30¾″. (Phyllis Haders; photograph courtesy America Hurrah Antiques)

155 (opposite, above). Crib quilt, Feathered Star with Sawtooth border, Pennsylvania, 1880–1890. 40″ x 40″. The quilting is particularly fine on this small piece. A vase of flowers is the center motif, and four hearts are quilted in each of the stars. (Bill Gallick and Tony Ellis)

156 (opposite, below). Pieced and appliqué quilt, Alphabet, New York, dated 1871. 74″ x 60½″. (Thos. K. Woodard: American Antiques & Quilts)

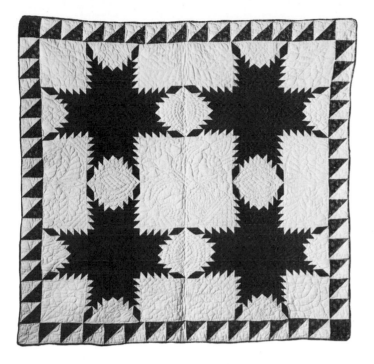

CHILDREN'S WORLD

There was a time when most girls of five years or older had already begun their instruction in the art of sewing and quiltmaking. Early accounts relate how a single block was stitched and taken apart and restitched until a sufficient degree of competency had been reached. Then several blocks were fashioned and ultimately combined to form a quilt top. Generally, pieced quilt tops were worked first; the more difficult appliqués were not attempted until skills were more fully developed. While dutiful children continued to improve their needlework, their loving elders made miniature quilts for cribs and children's beds. The miniature quilt, popularly known today as the crib quilt, often displays masterful design and extraordinary technique.

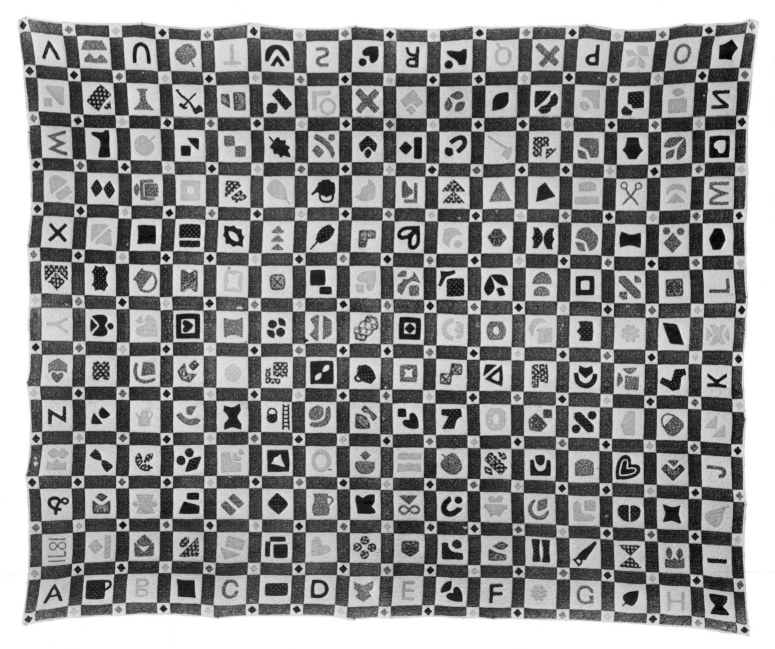

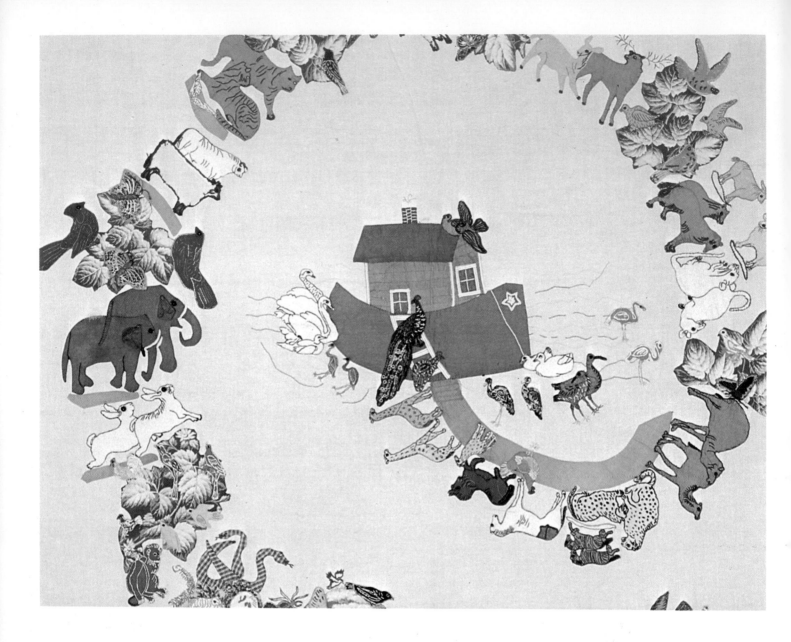

157 (left), 157a (above). Appliqué quilt showing Noah's Ark with all the animals, 1870–1880. 75½" x 78½". Made to delight a child, this enchanting quilt would also help him to identify many different animals and to count them—two by two. The late nineteenth-century printed fabrics are particularly interesting. (Mr. and Mrs. Foster McCarl, Jr.)

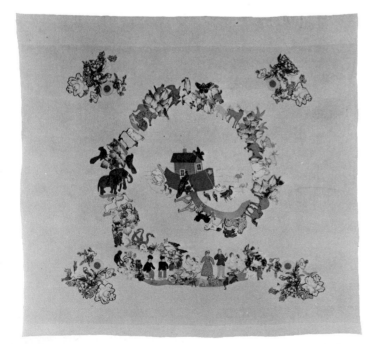

158 (below). Pieced and appliqué child's quilt, 1940. 60″ x 48″. This sprightly menagerie was imaginatively created from fabrics of unusual patterns and colors. The blocks with the animals are also embellished with embroidery. (Dahlov Ipcar)

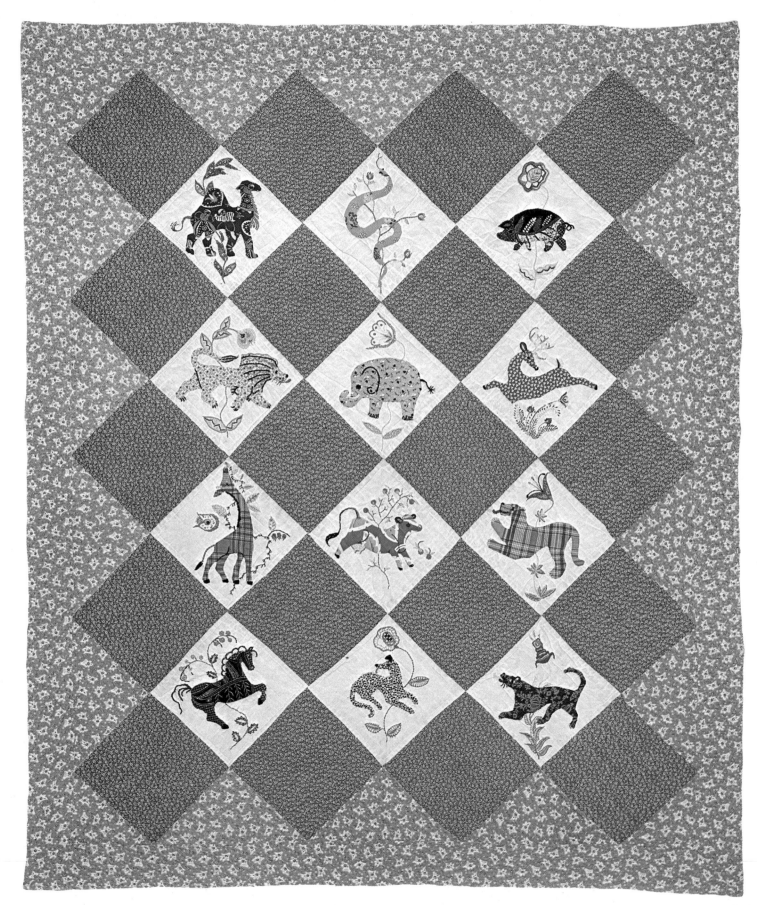

"Little girls often find amusement in making patchwork quilts for the beds of their dolls, and some even go so far as to make cradle quilts for their infant brothers and sisters," reported *Godey's Lady's Book* in January, 1835.

While the patchwork crib quilt might delight both child and adult in country areas, probably few were as "tasteful" as the ornately embroidered "Cover for a Baby's Crib" described by Almon C. Varney in 1884: "There was recently shown at the rooms of the Society of Decorative Art in New York, a crib cover which attracted great attention. The material was worked with silk, on white linen, the design, in outline being several sleepy birds perched upon a branch, with a motto underneath—'Little babes which sleep all night/Laugh in the face of sorrow;/Little birds which sleep all night/Sing carols on the morrow.'"[18]

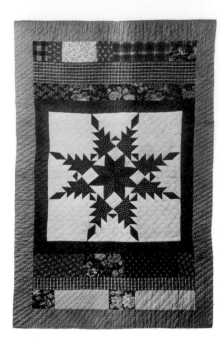

159 (right). Pieced crib quilt, Feathered Star enclosing Lemoyne Star, Connecticut, c. 1865. 49½″ x 42½″. (Phyllis Haders)

160 (below). Interior of Luther Burbank's birthplace. Before the fireplace stands a cradle that Luther's father made for his infant son. (Greenfield Village and Henry Ford Museum)

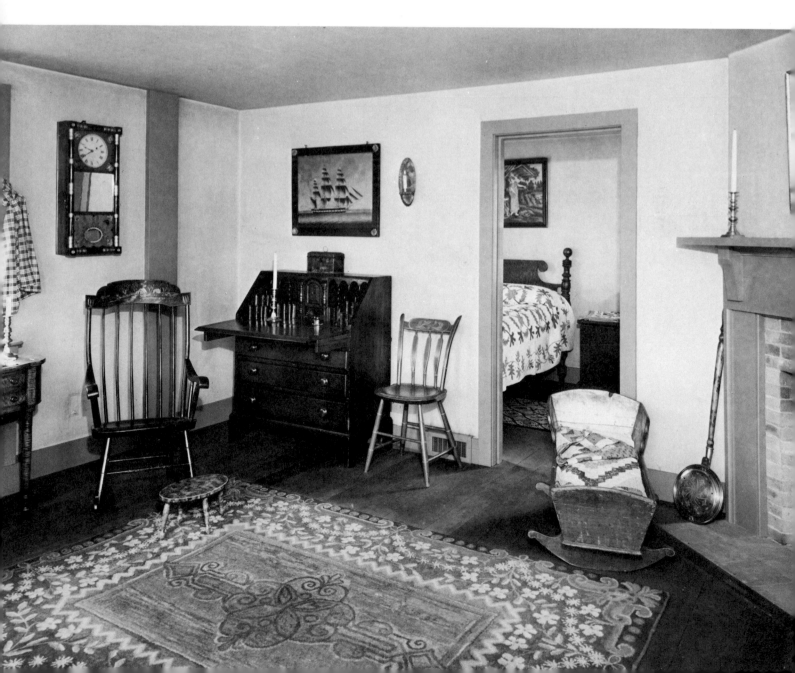

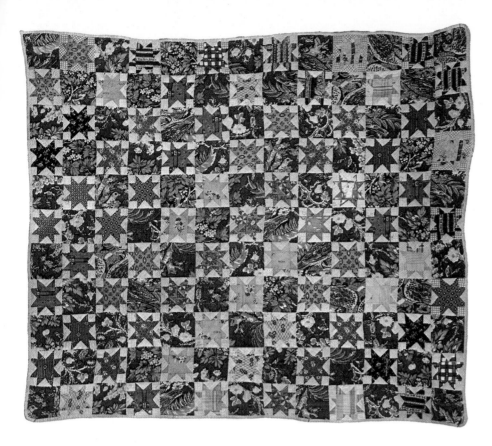

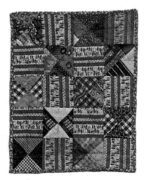

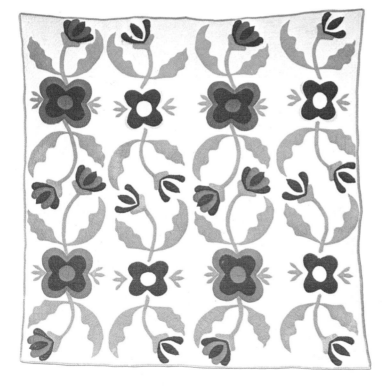

163 (above, right). Pieced doll's quilt, Broken Dishes, New England, c. 1845. 14¼" x 11½". (America Hurrah Antiques)

164 (below). Pieced and appliqué crib quilt top, c. 1875. 44" x 43". Without question, this extraordinary piece is unique among crib quilts. It glitters with imaginative design and rich color. A magnifying glass will show the similarity between the printed fabrics used for the human and animal figures in this piece and those used in figure 157, page 106. (America Hurrah Antiques)

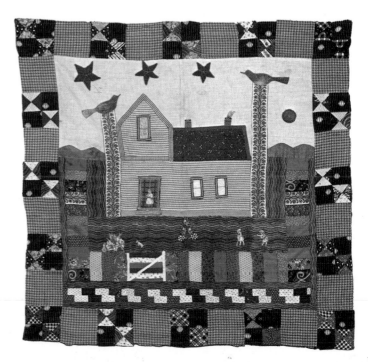

161 (top, left). Pieced crib quilt, Variable Star, New England, c. 1840. 34½" x 39¾". (American Hurrah Antiques)

162 (above). Appliqué crib quilt, variation of Ohio Rose, Pennsylvania, c. 1850. 43½" x 41½". The designs on crib quilts are generally quite small. The large flowers and leaves on this piece are unusual. (Mr. and Mrs. Foster McCarl, Jr.)

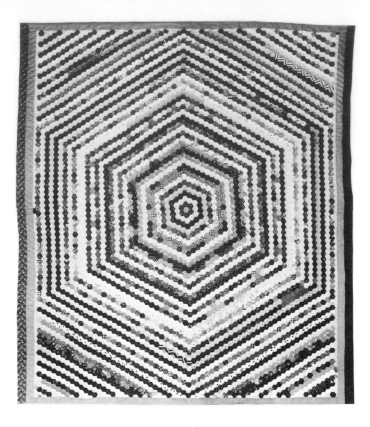

165 (left). Pieced quilt, Mosaic, made by Susan McCord, Indiana, 1840–1850. 84″ x 76″. Mrs. McCord named this quilt Grandmother's Garden. It is made of three-quarter-inch hexagonal patches that have been pieced in concentric hexagonal rings. The borders are red and green calico. (Greenfield Village and Henry Ford Museum)

166 (below). The McCord family sitting in front of their farm at McCordsville, Indiana. Left to right: Mrs. Millie Cannaday (Mrs. McCord's daughter); Green McCord (Mrs. McCord's husband); Ruth Cannaday (Millie's daughter and Susan's granddaughter); Susan McCord. (Greenfield Village and Henry Ford Museum)

167 (opposite, above). Crazy quilt top, made by Susan McCord, Indiana, c. 1900. 80″ x 66″. This complex design is made up of various-sized fans that are sometimes juxtaposed to form wheels. Many of the wool patches are joined with featherstitched embroidery. (Greenfield Village and Henry Ford Museum)

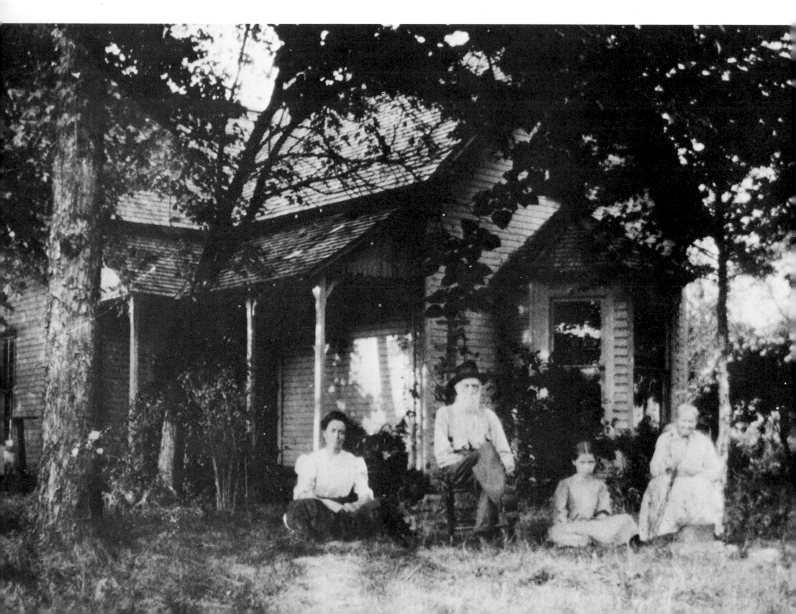

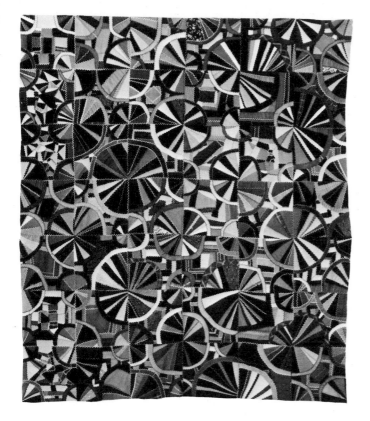

SUSAN McCORD'S LEGACY

Old accounts often tell us of a staggering number of quilts that were made by a single needlewoman. Dr. William R. Dunton, Jr., writing in 1934, recalled the work of Mrs. Julia Ann Flickinger, who was born January 8, 1827. "From the moment when she was old enough to wield needle and thread, she must have been an industrious piecer of quilts, for, at her death, she left over one hundred and fifty.[19]

All of the quilts shown in these four pages were made by Susan McCord. They form an interesting study collection, for they were made over an extended period of time and indicate the changing tastes of Victorian America.

A great-granddaughter of Mrs. McCord has written: "Mrs. Susan McCord was born October 7, 1829 . . . On August 2, 1849, she and Green McCord were united in marriage at Greensburg, Indiana. After that eventful day, both she and her husband settled down on a farm in the McCordsville area. Mrs. McCord, a woman of slightly over five feet tall, did all her own household duties in addition to making butter and soap and performing other chores on the farm. Every year she put out a big garden and canned and dried fruits and vegetables. She was also active in the Methodist Church and was faithful in reading her Bible through every year . . . Mrs. McCord also displayed remarkable ability in the textile field. One marvels that she had the time to do such work, but she was a person who had to be busy even during idle moments. Quilting was one of her hobbies. At quilting bees, the women would exchange quilt patterns and ideas. Mrs. McCord utilized scraps and remnants of her children's and grandchildren's clothing for her many quilts. . . . Then she was also adept in her embroidery work. She did lovely silk embroidery on shawls and steel bead embroidery on satin handbags. In the embroidery line, she exhibited a unique idea—that of embroidering in red two sheets to be used as bedspreads. Photographs in almanacs, magazines, newspapers, and seed catalogs picturing flowers were her inspiration for undertaking this task. She drew her own patterns from these pictures . . . Of course, she had no idea that much of her textile work would appear in museums for posterity to see and enjoy. Undoubtedly Mrs. McCord lived a rich, full life. At the ripe age of eighty years, a domestic accident occurred. A cow kicked her over, breaking a hip. Death came on December 12, 1909. Thus ended life on earth for Mrs. Susan McCord, but the world is richer for her having been here."[20]

These enthusiastic reminiscences do not adequately acknowledge Susan McCord's significant contribution to the history of American needlework. She deserves to be considered as important in her field as America's finest folk painters are in theirs.

168 (below). Appliqué quilt, Whig Rose and Urn, made by Susan McCord, Indiana, c. 1850. 82" x 76". The border is composed of a vine with a different floral motif on each of the four sides. (Greenfield Village and Henry Ford Museum)

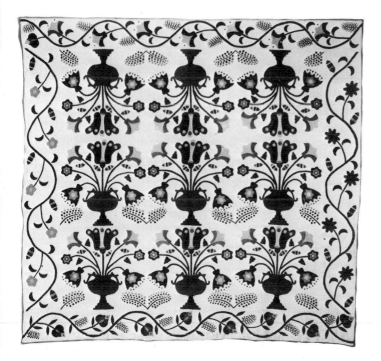

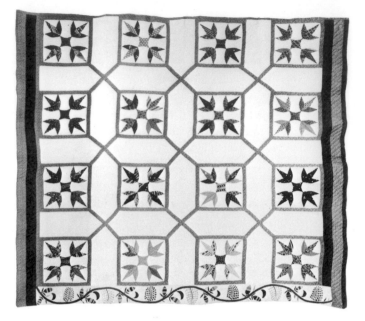

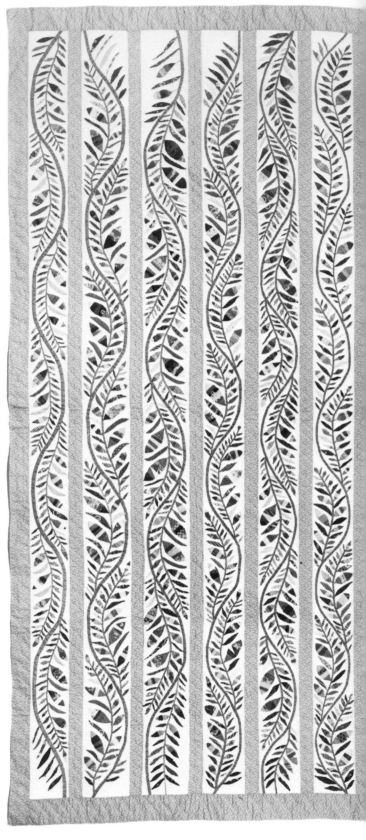

169 (above). Pieced quilt, Turkey Tracks or Wandering Foot, made by Susan McCord, Indiana. c. 1840. 82″ x 72″. The bottom border is made up of undulating vines with flowers and grape clusters quilted in a feather pattern. Mrs. McCord was particularly fond of this design, and it appears on many of her quilts. (Greenfield Village and Henry Ford Museum)

170 (below). Pieced and appliqué quilt, Ocean Waves, made by Susan McCord, Indiana, 1850–1860. 72″ x 72″. The central design contains thousands of half-inch triangular patches snipped from many different printed fabrics. (Greenfield Village and Henry Ford Museum)

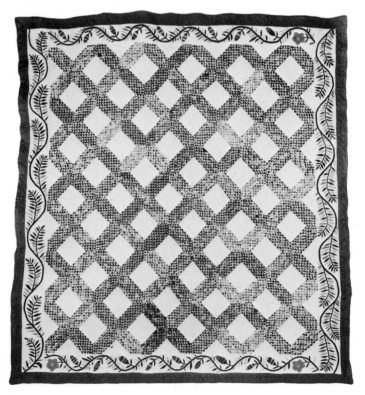

171 (above), 171a (opposite). Pieced and appliqué quilt in a vine design divided by sets. Made by Susan McCord, Indiana, c. 1845. 80″ x 76″. Study this quilt closely to appreciate fully not only the beauty of the conception, but also the sheer labor involved in

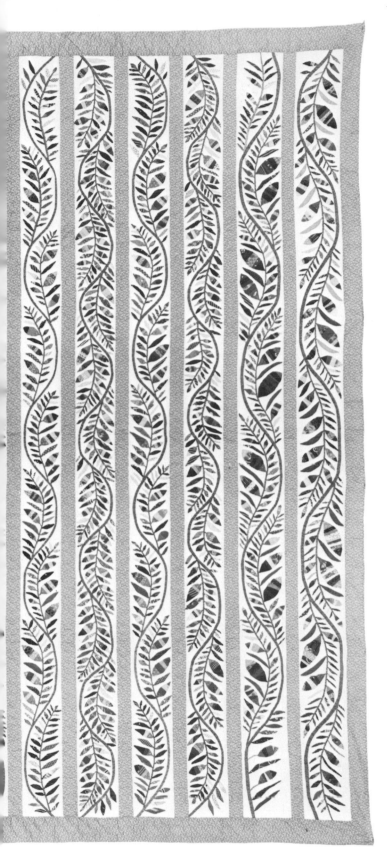

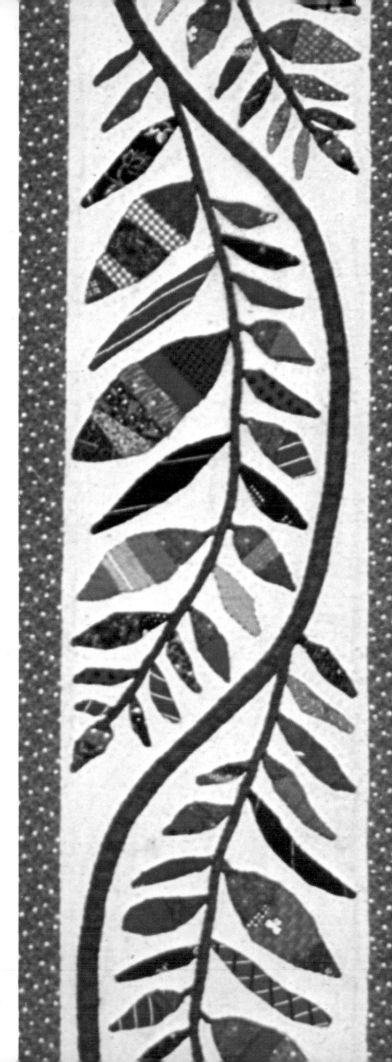

piecing together the clustered "flowers" depending from
the vines. The enlarged color detail on page 113
shows clearly the splendor of the needlework. The
result is one of the most magnificent quilts known.
(Greenfield Village and Henry Ford Museum)

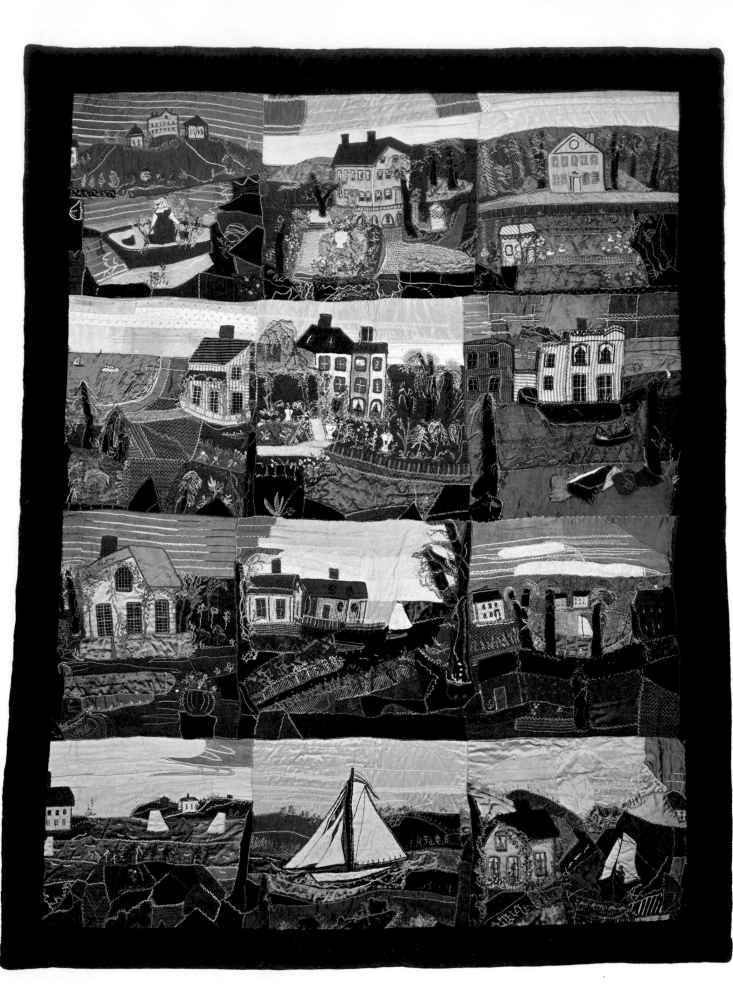

THE CRAZY QUILT

Many believe that the constant patching of worn-out clothes inspired some imaginative housewife to develop the idea of a crazy quilt. The earliest of these utilitarian bedcovers were probably secured by tying or "tufting" the top, the stuffing, and the back at regular intervals.

The fad for the crazy quilt reached its peak during the Victorian period. Its overwrought style perfectly suited the nineteenth-century love of sentiment, for treasured hair ribbons, bits of mother's wedding dress, and even men's neckties and bathing suits could be incorporated into the piece. Elaborate cotton or silk embroidery dressed up a commonplace piece and made it outright fashionable. However, crazy quilts were seldom quilted; most were probably used as showy parlor throws.

At the Philadelphia Centennial in 1876 a Japanese house and related displays sparked a taste for anything and everything Oriental. The popular Victorian writer, Almon C. Varney, perfectly reflected the fervor for such exotica in his article, "Japanese Piecework." "Collect a quantity of scraps and ribbon, brocade, satin, velvet, plush, and silk. If the pieces are small and odd in shape, so much the better. Take squares of old muslin, lay over them a half thickness of wadding, then baste on the pieces, turning in or covering the edges. Put them on in as fantastic a way as possible. Many embroider the larger spaces with palettes, crescents, arrows, butterflies, two rings interlocked, or any odd design, and cover all the seams with feather stitch or point *russe* . . ."[21]

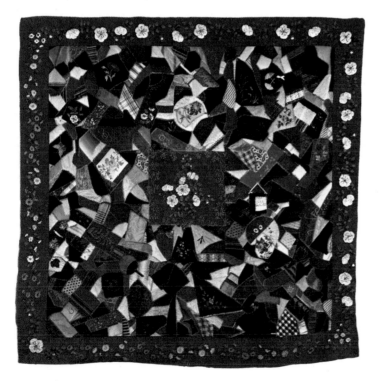

172 (opposite). Pieced and embroidered crazy quilt made by Celestine Bacheller, Wyoma, Massachusetts, c. 1900. 73½" x 57". The scenes in this superb piece are said to represent actual landscapes and houses near Wyoma. (Museum of Fine Arts, Boston; Gift of Mr. and Mrs. Edward J. Healy in memory of Mrs. Charles O'Malley)

173 (above). Crazy quilt with center medallion, made by Nettie Milam between 1876 and 1883, Cincinnati, Ohio. 64" x 62". (Cincinnati Art Museum; Gift of Mrs. V. M. Kunkel).

174 (below). Crazy quilt, made by Helen Mary Rounsville, Fowlerville, Michigan, c. 1887. 64" x 50". The quilt is made of velvets, silks, sateens, and silk embroidery thread. The horses are velvet appliqués with embroidered manes and tails and glass beads for the eyes. The flowers are beautifully worked. (Mary Strickler's Quilt Gallery)

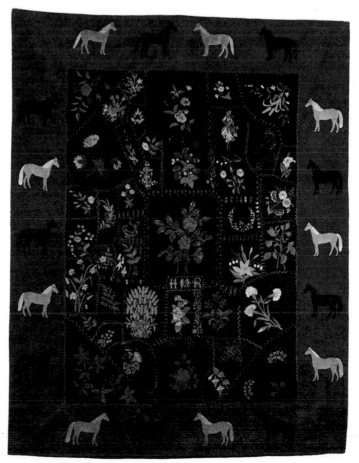

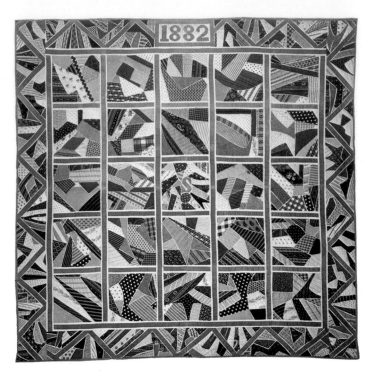

175 (above). Crazy quilt, Maine, dated 1882. 78¾" x 78½".
Contained crazy quilts are unsusual, and this example is
strikingly organized within squares and triangles. The color
range is also most effective. (Thos. K. Woodard:
American Antiques & Quilts)

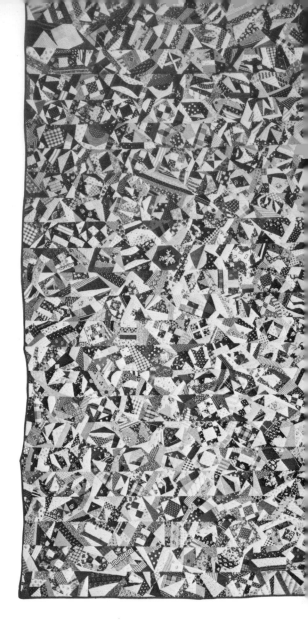

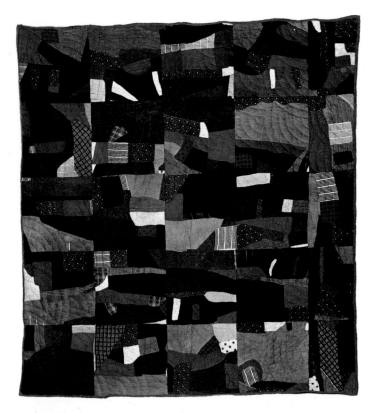

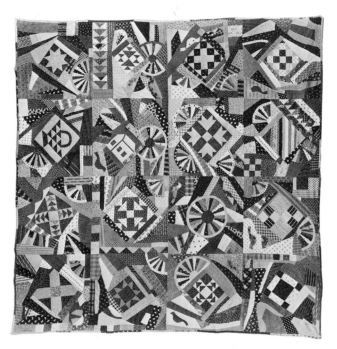

176 (above). Crazy quilt, Lancaster, Pennsylvania, area,
1900–1910. 78" x 73". Created from pieces of wool and
flannel and quilted in an arch design by a country woman,
this "crazy" shows an intuitive sense of the power of abstract
design and color that is very modern. (Private collection;
photograph courtesy America Hurrah Antiques)

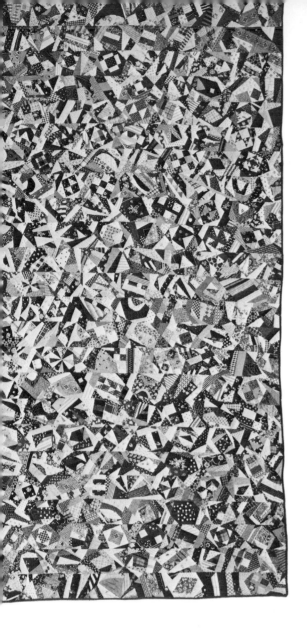

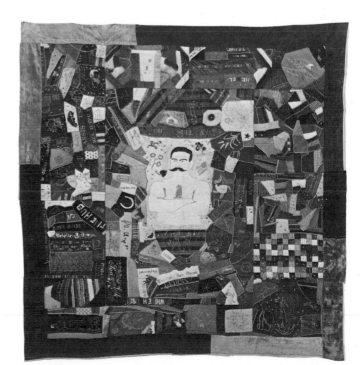

177 (above). Crazy quilt, Connecticut, 1885–1895.
87½″ x 75½″. This jigsaw puzzle of a quilt deserves close study
fully to appreciate the ingenuity of its organization. Basically,
it consists of long horizontal strips sewn together, but the
strips are, in turn, made up of elongated diamonds created
from the small fabric patches. If all that wasn't enough,
the quiltmaker decided to prove how really clever she was
and included here and there a few pieced-quilt designs.
It is an astonishing performance. (America Hurrah Antiques)

178 (opposite, below right). Crazy quilt, Vermont, c. 1885.
76½″ x 76½″. This very effective "crazy" has been organized
into large blocks incorporating familiar pieced-quilt designs
in addition to the irregular patches. (Thos. K. Woodard:
American Antiques & Quilts)

179 (right), 179a (above, right). Crazy quilt, Illinois, dated
1888. 79″ x 76″. Like the majority of crazy quilts, this
amusing tribute to the great boxer John L. Sullivan glows
with richly colored scraps of silk and velvet. Sullivan is shown
fighting with Kilrain directly below his embroidered portrait.
Scattered throughout the quilt are the needleworked logos
of Chicago papers of the period. It seems safe to assume that
this luxurious spread was made for a man. (Betty Sterling)

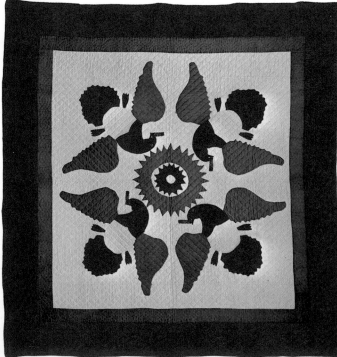

180 (above). Appliqué quilt, one of a pair, Ohio, 1860–1870. 86¾″ x 83″. Sprightly color and good design make this patriotic spread particularly appealing. It is rare to find a pair of quilts. (John Bihler and Henry Coger)

181 (below). Appliqué quilt, Pennsylvania, 1885–1895. 82″ x 80″. This type of quilt featuring four eagles became very popular after the Philadelphia Centennial Exposition. The quiltmaker has given her eagles a rather swaggering aspect, since they appear to be smoking cigars! (America Hurrah Antiques)

AMERICA IN QUILTS

Some of the most colorful and meaningful American quilts are those that have been inspired by the patriotism of their makers. Since America's Bicentennial Year will soon be celebrated, it seems appropriate to close this book with illustrations of a number of fine patriotic quilts, with Mary Borkowski's Bicentennial quilt, *Spirit of '76*, which symbolizes a united America, being the last quilt in the book.

All the familiar symbols of the United States are to be found in these quilts. Washington, "The Father of His Country," appears with Martha in figure 186, and is seen with his horse in the center of the great Centennial quilt in figure 191. The national flag waves bravely in figure 182, forms the background of figure 186, and is used to keep "Baby" warm in figure 185. The eagle, which is, of course, prominent in many of the quilts, was adopted as a national symbol over the objections of Benjamin Franklin, who thought that the wild turkey was far more appropriate. All of the design elements of the superb quilt in figure 187 focus attention on the eagle and national motto *E Pluribus Unum* in the center.

183 (below). Appliqué quilt, Pennsylvania, initialed LW and dated 1844. 75″ x 67″. Eagles, hearts, and stars scintillate in this strong example of folk art. The colors are blue and white. (Adirondack Memories)

182 (above). Pieced and appliqué quilt, Freedom Album, New England, c. 1855. One eagle, two shields, and three flags combine effectively with a variety of other designs in this coverlet. (Langehorn and Judy Washburn; photograph courtesy America Hurrah Antiques)

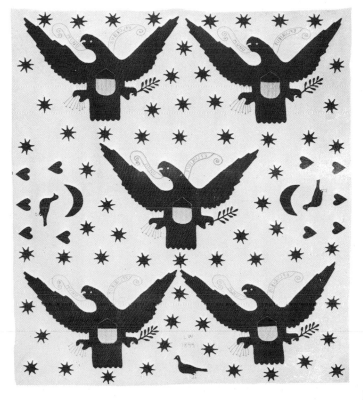

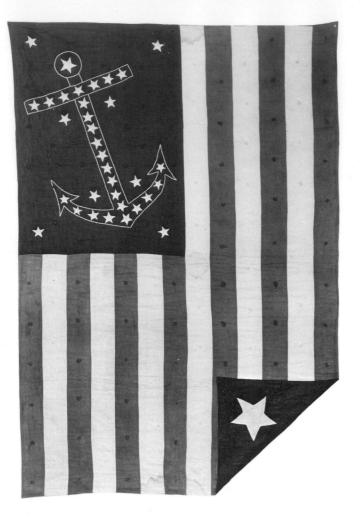

184 (left). Pieced and appliqué quilt shown with the corner turned back. It was made during the Civil War for a Union officer from Rhode Island. 78″ x 54″. Four stars and the initials GCO are appliquéd on the reverse. The stars have the following penned inscriptions: "God bless the Union army and the flag by which it stands. God bless our stars forever"; "One flag, one land, one nation evermore. Where breathes the foe but falls before us"; "Never falter while there's treason abroad. Union and Liberty one evermore"; "Strike till the last armed foe expires. Up up with your banner for God and the right." (Private collection; photograph courtesy America Hurrah Antiques)

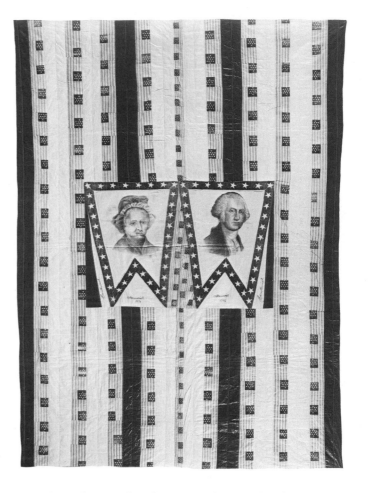

185 (below). Pieced and appliqué crib quilt, Kansas, c. 1861. 36¾″ x 36″. The word "Baby" is embroidered in the center of the rather lopsided blue star. (Phyllis Haders)

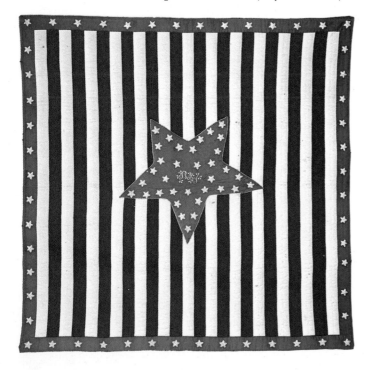

186 (above). Pieced quilt, New York state, dated 1876. 75½″ x 54¼″. The portraits of George and Martha Washington are printed black. The red, white, and blue background fabric to which they are stitched is polished cotton in a repeat pattern of American flags. The quilt is inscribed "Centennial Memorial" on the portraits. (Adirondack Memories)

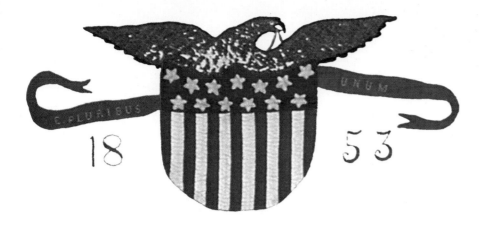

187 (below), 187a (left). Pieced and appliqué quilt, dated 1853. 86¼″ x 85″. One could not hope to find a more impressive example of color, design, and needlework combined in one glorious quilt. Each of the pieced stars is embroidered in the center with the name of one of the thirteen original Colonies: New Hampshire, Massachusetts, Rhode Island, Connecticut, New York, New Jersey, Delaware, Pennsylvania, Maryland, Virginia, North Carolina, South Carolina, and Georgia. (Cora Ginsburg)

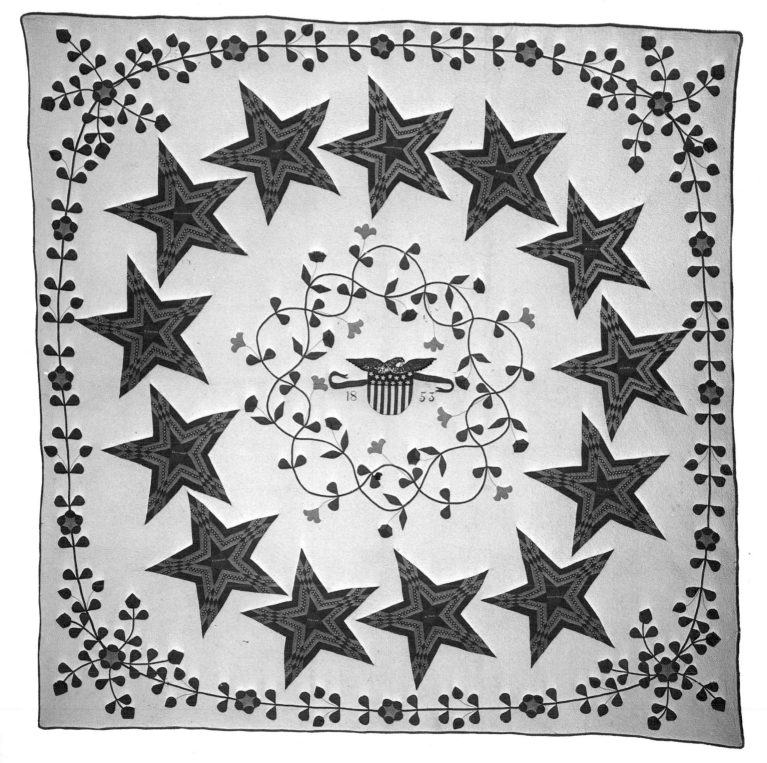

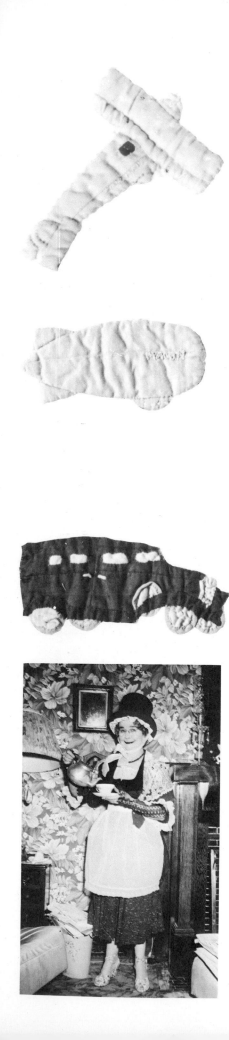

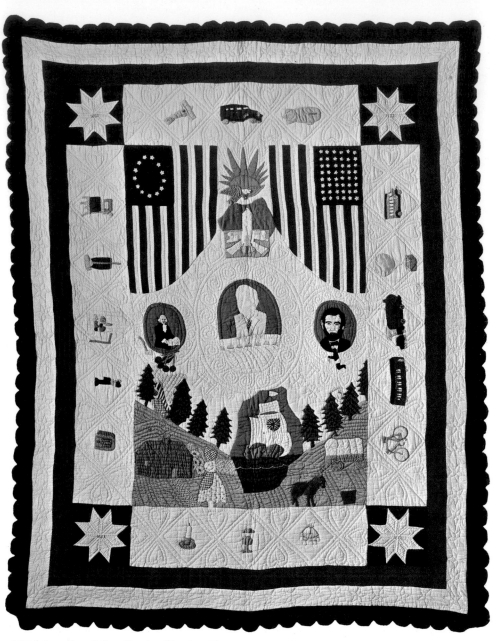

188 (above) and details. Appliqué quilt commemorating the Century of Progress Exhibition of 1933, made by Mrs. W. B. Lathouse of Warren, Ohio. 82″ x 66″. The unfinished portrait between Washington and Lincoln is Franklin Delano Roosevelt. (America Hurrah Antiques)

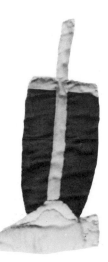

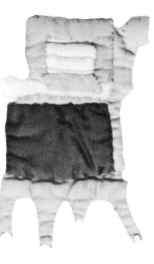

189 (opposite, below left). Mrs. Lathouse, a professional seamstress born in Wales, came to the United States in 1922. She is seen here in her native Welsh costume. (Photograph courtesy America Hurrah Antiques)

190 (below). Appliqué Victory quilt, made by Mrs. Lathouse in 1945. 88" x 74". Mrs. Lathouse was obviously a very patriotic woman. The portraits show Stalin, Churchill, Roosevelt, and MacArthur. The American eagle is ripping the Nazi and Japanese flags, and the Russian bear and English bulldog are also included. The pansies at the top are a symbol of remembrance. The three dots and a dash represent the letter V (for victory) in Morse code. (America Hurrah Antiques)

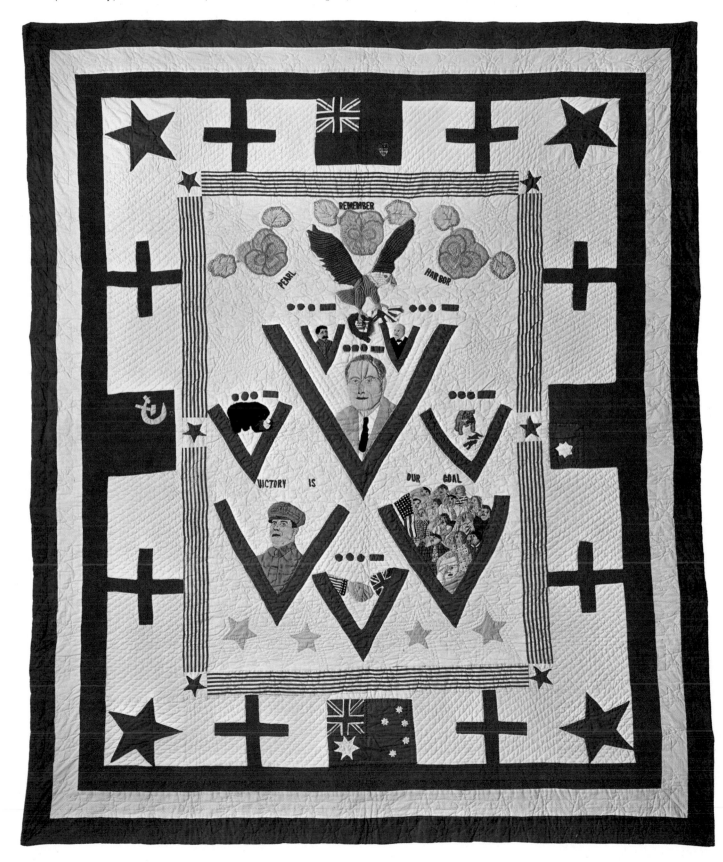

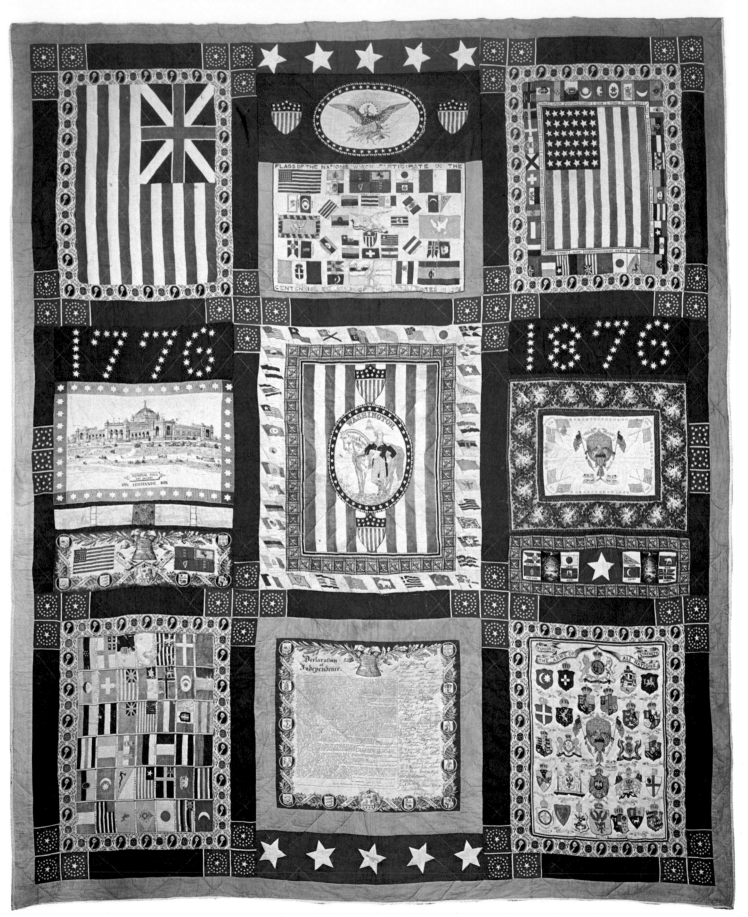

191 (above). Pieced Centennial quilt, c. 1876. 104″ x 83″. This stunning quilt is made up of commemorative squares of printed fabric sold as souvenirs at the time of the Philadelphia Centennial in 1876. Washington and his horse are in the center, and directly underneath is the Declaration of Independence. (Judith Pedersen and John McElhatton; photograph courtesy Phyllis and Sidney Rosner)

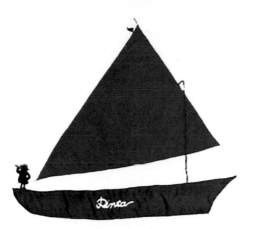

192 (below), 192a (left). Pieced and appliqué Bicentennial quilt, *Spirit of '76*, made by Mary Borkowski of Dayton, Ohio, in October, 1974. 111″ x 103″. Although the central motif of this fascinating quilt resembles a huge Variable Star, the maker says that it actually shows four figures clasping hands. They represent Americans standing together in a common cause. At the top are Columbus's three ships: the Niña, the Pinta, and the Santa Maria. The white background is quilted in a wave pattern. (Mr. and Mrs. William Burger; photograph courtesy Fairtree Gallery)

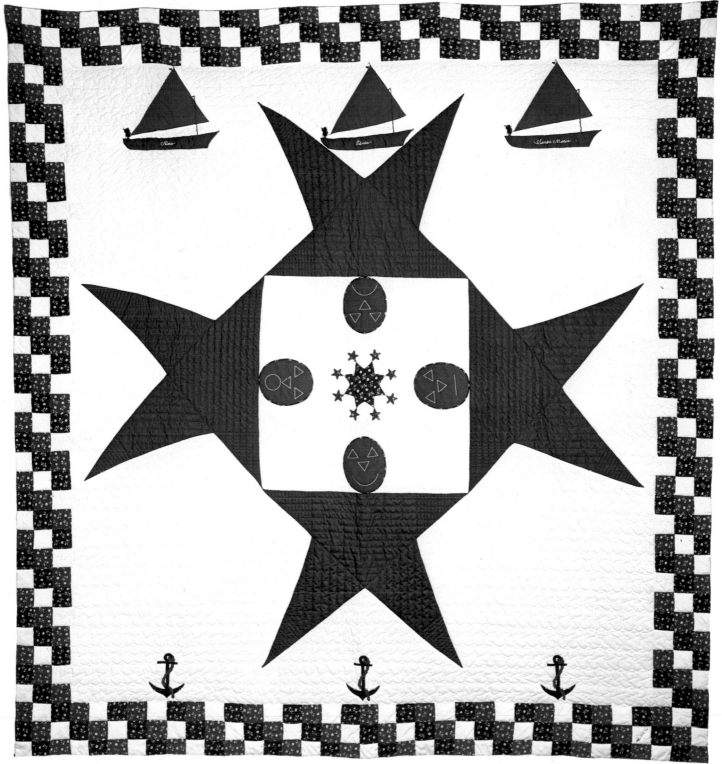

NOTES

1. Partial quote from George Francis Dow, *Every Day Life in the Massachusetts Bay Colony* (Boston: The Society for the Preservation of New England Antiquities, 1935. Reprinted, New York: Benjamin Blom., Inc.), p. 83.

2. Frances Trollope, *Domestic Manners of the Americans*, ed. Donald Smalley (New York: Vintage Books, 1949), p. 414.

3. Jonathan Holstein, *The Pieced Quilt: An American Design Tradition* (Greenwich, Conn.: New York Graphic Society Ltd., 1973), pp. 7–8.

4. Trollope, *Domestic Manners of the Americans*, p. 416.

5. "The Quilting at Miss Jones's," *Godey's Lady's Book*, January, 1868.

6. Marion Nicholl Rawson, *When Antiques Were Young* (New York: E. P. Dutton & Co., Inc., 1931), p. 129.

7. Carrie A. Hall and Rose G. Kretsinger, *The Romance of the Patchwork Quilt in America* (Caldwell, Idaho: Caxon Printers Ltd., 1935. Reprinted, New York: Bonanza Books), p. 36.

8. *Records of Ft. St. George; Despatches from England, 1681–86*. Partial quote in *Antiques* (October, 1969), p. 546.

9. Edward Baines, *History of the Cotton Manufacture in Great Britain* (London, 1836).

10. Patsy and Myron Orlofsky, *Quilts in America* (New York: McGraw-Hill Book Company, 1974), p. 79.

11. *Pennsylvania Gazette*, July, 1788.

12. Richard Schorleyker, *A Scholo-House for the Needle* (London, 1632).

13. Asa Ellis, Jr., *The Country Dyer's Assistant* (Brookfield, Mass., 1798), pp. 137–139.

14. *Scientific American*, March 18, 1892.

15. Mary Schenck Woolman, *A Sewing Course* (Washington, D.C.: Frederick A. Fernall, 1911), pp. 31–32.

16. Charles E. Bentley, "Decorative Art Needle-Work," *Our Homes and Their Adornments* (Detroit, Mich.: J. C. Chilton & Co., 1884)

17. Henry David Thoreau, *Walden or, Life in the Woods*, 1854. (Reprinted, New York: New American Library, 1960), pp. 82–83.

18. Almon C. Varney, *Our Homes and Their Adornments* (Detroit, Mich.: J. C. Chilton & Co., 1884), p. 351.

19. *Antiques* (August, 1934), p. 36.

20. Unpublished manuscript in the collection of Greenfield Village and Henry Ford Museum, Dearborn, Michigan.

21. Varney, *Our Homes and Their Adornments*, p. 273.

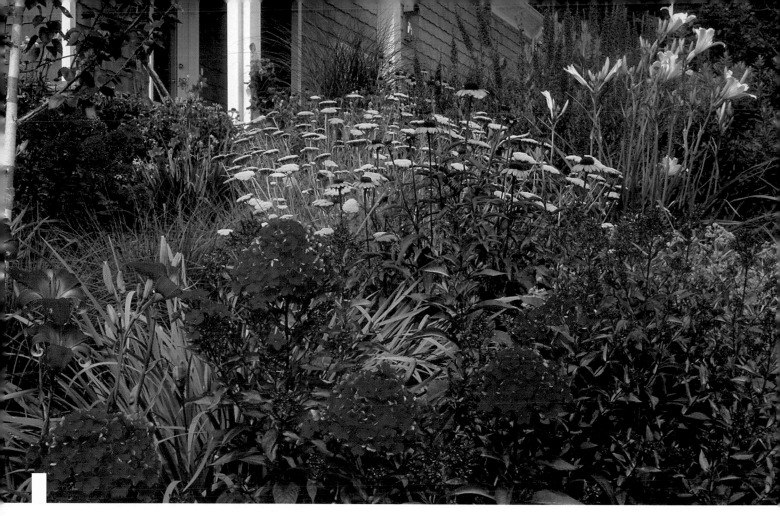

Still, challenges do exist—namely, heavy soil and wild weather—and to create a beautiful garden that has some stamina, you'll need to work with those givens.

REGIONAL INFLUENCES

As a Midwesterner born and raised, I'd always assumed that good garden soil was my birthright. I grew up in the suburbs, but just down the road was a real working farm where

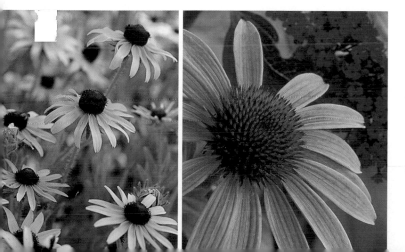

Farmer Olson grew corn. He liked to point out that the Midwest has the finest topsoil on the planet. But he never talked about how difficult farming was before the steel plow came along. Early settlers had to use special cutting tools just to get through the tangle of weeds and grasses, then hand-till the heavy, albeit mineral-rich soil underneath. Nor did he say that what works for farm crops doesn't necessarily work for most garden plants, which have relatively delicate roots that can't penetrate dense soil. Steel plows and hand-tilling won't suffice. Gardeners must routinely add sand, leaf mold, and compost to lighten the soil.

Onerous as all this sounds, gardening in the Midwest is no worse than gardening in places where the soil is rocky or infertile or hopelessly

Gardening in the Midwest

Midwestern gardeners are so used to hearing experts describe our region as the land of extremes, a place other than the norm, where this or that will not grow, we sometimes forget to count our blessings. Peonies love our bracing climate, whereas they collapse in southern humidity and won't grow at all in subtropical regions. Tulips are another cold-climate plant: they need to spend a few weeks in near-freezing temperatures or they won't bloom again. While it's true that we have more than our share of obnoxious weeds, at least our winters help keep the more rampant thugs in check—along with beautiful but potentially invasive plants like wisteria. Cold winters combined with our relative dryness also allow many rock-garden plants that are native to mountainous regions like the high Alps to live outdoors here all year, while they must be kept in artificially cooled and dehumidified greenhouses to survive in Britain's soggy weather. And while we can't grow giant rhododendrons like gardeners can in Seattle's more moderate climate, we don't have slugs as big as theirs either.

OPPOSITE PAGE: *Masses of colorful annual zinnias drink in the full sun of an Iowa cutting garden.*

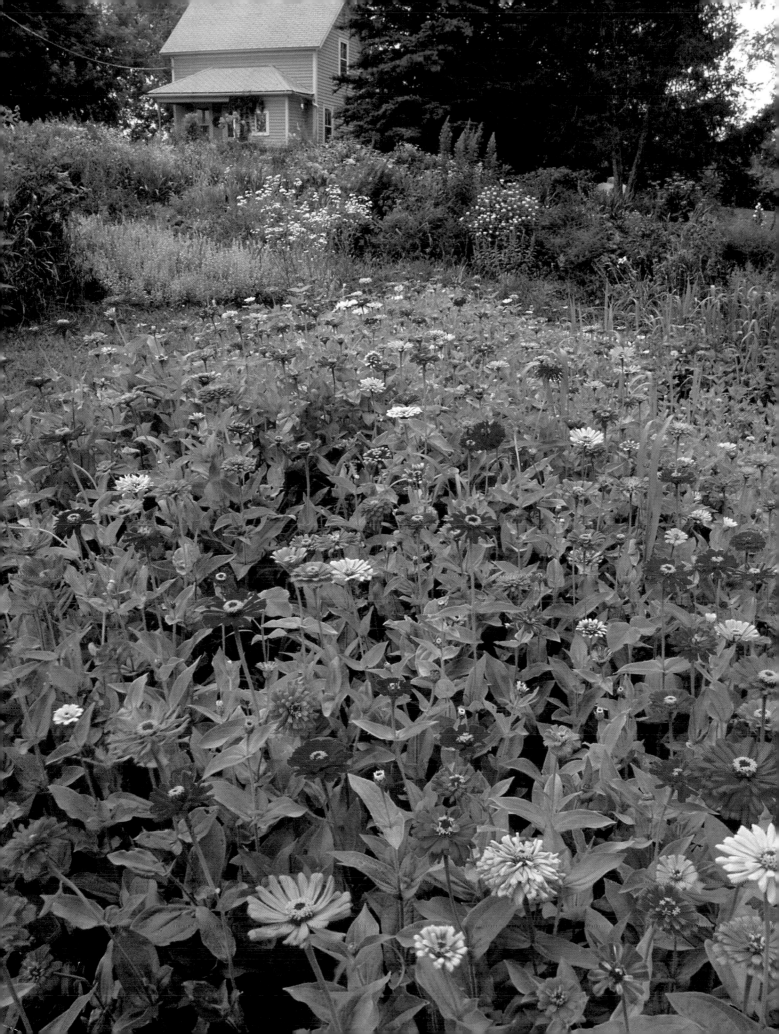

Contents

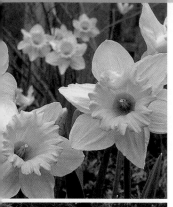

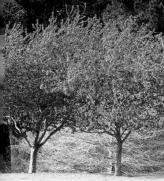

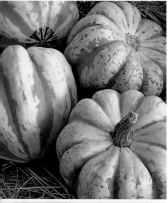

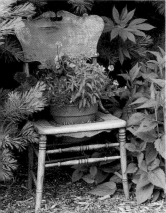

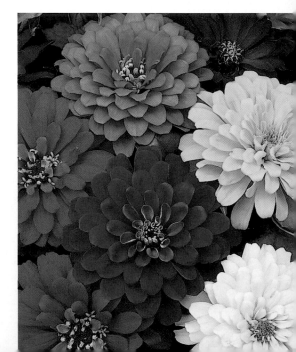

SELECTED BIBLIOGRAPHY

Bacon, Lenice. *American Patchwork Quilts.* New York: William Morrow & Co., Inc., 1973.

Beer, Alice Baldwin. *Trade Goods, A Study of Indian Chintz.* Washington, D.C.: Smithsonian Institution Press, 1970.

Carlisle, Lilian Baker. *Quilts at Shelburne Museum.* Shelburne, Vt.: Shelburne Museum Publication, 1957.

Colby, Averil. *Patchwork.* New York: B. T. Batsford, 1958.

———. *Quilting.* New York: Charles Scribner's Sons, 1971.

Comstock, Helen, ed. *The Concise Encyclopedia of American Antiques.* New York: Hawthorn Books, Inc., 1958.

Creekmore, Betsy B. *Traditional American Crafts.* Knoxville, Tenn.: Hearthside Press, Inc., 1968.

Cummings, Abbott Lowell. *Bed Hangings.* Boston: Society for the Preservation of New England Antiquities, 1961.

Davis, Mildred J. *The Art of Crewel Embroidery.* New York: Crown Publishers, Inc., 1962.

———. *Early American Embroidery Designs.* New York: Crown Publishers, Inc., 1969.

———. *Embroidery Designs 1780 Through 1820.* New York: Crown Publishers, Inc., 1971.

Dunham, Lydia Roberts. "Denver Art Museum Quilt Collection." *Denver Art Museum Quarterly* (Winter 1963).

Earle, Alice Morse. *Customs & Fashions in Old New England.* 1893. Reprint. Williamstown, Mass.: Corner House, 1969.

Fennelly, Catherine. *Textiles in New England 1790–1840.* Sturbridge, Mass.: Old Sturbridge Village, 1961.

Finley, Ruth. *Old Patchwork Quilts and the Women Who Made Them.* 1929. Reprinted. Philadelphia: J. B. Lippincott, 1946.

Gammell, Alice I. *Polly Prindle's Book of American Patchwork.* New York: Grosset & Dunlap, Inc., 1973.

Giffen, Jane C. "Household Textiles, a Review." *Historical New Hampshire,* Vol. 22, No. 4 (1971).

Gutcheon, Beth. *The Perfect Patchwork Primer.* New York: David McKay Co., Inc., 1973.

Hall, Carrie A., and Kretsinger, Rose G. *The Romance of the Patchwork Quilt in America.* Caldwell, Idaho: Caxton Printers, Ltd., 1935. Reprinted. New York: Bonanza Books.

Hinson, Dolores. *Quilting Manual.* Knoxville, Tenn.: Hearthside Press, Inc., 1970.

———. *A Quilter's Companion.* New York: Arco Publishing Co., Inc., 1973.

Holstein, Jonathan. *The Pieced Quilt: An American Tradition.* Greenwich, Conn.: New York Graphic Society, 1973.

Iverson, Marion Day. "Bed Rugs in Colonial America." *Antiques* (January 1964).

Katzenberg, Dena S. *The Great American Cover-Up: Counterpanes of the Eighteenth and Nineteenth Centuries.* Baltimore, Md.: Baltimore Museum of Art, 1971.

Laury, Jean Ray. *Quilts and Coverlets: A Contemporary Approach.* New York: Van Nostrand Reinhold Co., 1970.

Lewis, Alfred Allan. *The Mountain Artisans' Quilting Book.* New York: Macmillan Co., Inc., 1973.

Lithgow, Marilyn. *Quiltmaking and Quiltmakers.* New York: Funk & Wagnalls, 1974.

Lord, Priscilla Sawyer, and Foley, Daniel J. *The Folk Arts and Crafts of New England.* Philadelphia: Chilton Books, 1965.

MacIver, Percival. *The Chintz Book.* New York: Frederick A. Stokes Co., 1923.

Mahler, Celine. *Once Upon a Quilt: Patchwork Design and Technique.* New York: Van Nostrand Reinhold Co., 1973.

Marston, Doris E. *Exploring Patchwork.* Newton Center, Mass.: Charles T. Branford Co., 1972.

Martens, Rachel. *Modern Patchwork.* Garden City, N.Y.: Doubleday & Co., Inc., 1971.

Montgomery, Florence M. *Printed Textiles: English and American Cottons and Linens 1700–1850.* New York: The Viking Press, 1970.

Morris, Barbara. *Victorian Embroidery.* New York: Thomas Nelson and Sons, 1962.

Orlofsky, Patsy and Myron. *Quilts in America.* New York: McGraw-Hill Book Company, 1974.

Peto, Florence. *American Quilts and Coverlets.* New York: Chanticleer Press, 1949.

Preston, Paula Sampson. *Printed Cottons at Old Sturbridge Village.* Sturbridge, Mass.: Sturbridge Village Publication, 1969.

Safford, Carleton L., and Bishop, Robert. *America's Quilts and Coverlets.* New York: E. P. Dutton & Co., Inc., 1972.

Schiffer, Margaret B. *Historical Needlework of Pennsylvania.* New York: Charles Scribner's Sons, 1968.

Schwartz, Esther I. "Notes from a New Jersey Collector." *Antiques* (October 1958).

Quilting and Patchwork. Menlo Park, Calif.: Lane Magazine & Book Co., 1973.

Stevens, Napua. *The Hawaiian Quilt.* Honolulu: Service Printers, 1971.

Timmins, Alice. *Introducing Patchwork.* New York: Watson-Guptill Publications, Inc., 1968.

Warren, William L. *Bed Ruggs: 1722–1833.* Hartford, Conn.: Wadsworth Atheneum, 1972.

Webster, Marie D. *Quilts: Their Story and How to Make Them.* 1915. Reprinted. New York: Belmont-Tower Books, 1972.

White, Margaret E. *Quilts and Counterpanes in the Newark Museum.* Newark, N.J.: The Newark Museum Association, 1948.

Wooster, Ann-Sargent. *Quiltmaking.* New York: Drake Publishers, Inc., 1972.